P9-CCU-900

Kitchen Glassware
of the Depression Years
Fifth Edition

Gene Florence

COLLECTOR BOOKS
A Division of Schroeder Publishing Co., Inc.

The current values in this book should be used only as a guide. They are not intended to set prices, which vary from one section of the country to another. Auction prices as well as dealer prices vary greatly and are affected by condition as well as demand. Neither the Author nor the Publisher assumes responsibility for any losses that might be incurred as a result of consulting this guide.

SEARCHING FOR A PUBLISHER?

We are always looking for knowledeable people considered to be experts within their fields. If you feel that there is a real need for a book on your collectible subject and have a large comprehensive collection, contact Collector Books.

Additional copies of this book may be ordered from:

COLLECTOR BOOKS
P.O. Box 3009
Paducah, Kentucky 42002-3009
or

GENE FLORENCE

P.O. Box 22186
Lexington, Kentucky 40522

P.O. Box 64
Astatula, Florida 34705

Web Page: http://members.aol.com/GFlore829/GeneFlorence

Copyright: Gene Florence, 1995
Values Updated, 1997
This book or any part thereof may not be reproduced without the written consent of the Author and Publisher.

About The Author

Gene Florence, born in Lexington in 1944, graduated from the University of Kentucky where he held a double major in mathematics and English. He taught nine years in Kentucky at the junior high and high school levels before his glass collecting "hobby" became his full time job.

Mr. Florence has been interested in "collecting" since childhood, beginning with baseball cards and progressing through comic books, coins, bottles, and finally, glassware. He first became interested in Depression Glass after buying an entire set of Sharon dinnerware at a garage sale for $5.00.

He has written several books on glassware: The *Collector's Encyclopedia of Depression Glass*, now in its eleventh edition; *Elegant Glassware of the Depression Era*, now in its sixth edition; *The Collector's Encyclopedia of Akro Agate; The Collector's Encyclopedia of Occupied Japan*, Volumes I, II, III, IV and V; Very Rare Glassware of the Depression Years, (First, Second, Third and Fourth Series) and the *Pocket Guide to Depression Glass*, now in its ninth edition. He recently completed the fifth edition of his innovative Standard Baseball Card Price Guide that has been very well received in card collecting circles.

His 17-year-old Grannie Bear antique shop in Lexington, Ky., has now closed due to the sudden death of his mom, "Grannie Bear," who oversaw that store. Mr. Florence continues to sell glassware, however, via mail order and at Depression Glass shows throughout the country.

If you know of any **unlisted** or **unusual** pieces of kitchen glassware like the examples shown in this book, you may write Mr. Florence at Box 22186, Lexington, KY 40522. If you expect a reply, you must enclose a self-addressed, stamped envelope — and be patient. It is better to write him June through October since writing and researching three or four books each year leaves little time to answer the four to five thousand pieces of correspondence he receives.

Acknowledgments

A space of five years to re-examine the field of kitchenware was admittedly too long a time, but accumulating glassware not already shown in the previous books was a task. The sudden death of "Grannie Bear" prevented me from scheduling a trip to California to photograph some collections there for this book; but it couldn't be helped!

Many people assisted with this book by lending glass for photography on several occasions in the last few years. Pieces accumulated were photographed to add a page or two. Many thanks go to collectors from California to Florida who have offered opinions on pricing, but I have a special debt to Lorrie Kitchen, who not only helped price but spent extra hours searching for items priced that appear in more than one place in the book. All of us have attempted to make this book the finest in its field. Pictures shown herein were taken by photographers Dave Hammell from California, Richard Walker from New York, Kenn Whitmyer from Ohio, and Charley Lynch from Kentucky.

Thanks to the following for lending glass, or pricing information or help in photography: Dan Tucker and Lorrie Kitchen, Terry and Celia McDuffee, Dick and Pat Spencer, Hank and Carla Bowman, Sally Davis, Judy Smith, Stanley and Louise Duda, Sherry Harkins, Carrie Dormitz, Lenore Ewald, Bob and Carole Radcliffe, Edna Barnes, Arland and Marjorie Stokes, Melvin and Linda Sumter, Michelle Rosewitz, Jane White, Sherry Kraus, Lisa Stroup and numerous other collectors who have written me or shared information at shows for the benefit of fellow collectors.

My gratitude must be expressed to the editorial crew of Collector Books, Terri Stalions in particular, for help in putting this book together.

A heartfelt thanks is due the family, Cathy, Marc, Chad, and Becky Florence, and Charles and Sibyl Gaines who have superbly weathered the usual myriad ordeals of travel, shows, book orders and deadlines and the very unusual event of mother's death and the resulting gargantuan task of closing the shop!

Foreword

Availability of kitchenware, or the lack thereof, is the number one concern of collectors. In the five years since I wrote the fourth Kitchen Glassware of the Depression Years, I have been asked over and over, "When is the next book coming out?" Gathering wares for a new book is more like collecting than you think. Choice items for new pictures may be few and far between. We have added an additional 16 pages and eliminated as few photographs as absolutely necessary. I believe it is better to show an item not seen previously than to repeatedly show the same pieces. Please enjoy these 4,900 pieces of kitchenware! It's more than ever shown before, and getting them here was not an easy task! I hope you'll find all the effort taken worthwhile!

As with most collectibles, there are numerous pieces found over and over; but the already hard-to-find items show up less frequently. Exceptional pieces are bought by fervent collectors and until their particular collection is broken up or sold, many rarely found items are not offered again at any price. It takes patience as well as cash to collect. One of the joys of collecting is finding that specific piece that you have been pursuing for a long time. So many collectors have written or stopped by my booth at shows to express to me the joy they have received from collecting glass!

I have observed that more collectors are gathering kitchenware by colors than any other way. Because of this, **colors** are the first listing in this book with **items** and **patterns** following. I'm aware this causes some overlapping of photos and information.

Pricing

All prices in this book are retail prices for **mint condition** glassware. This book is intended to be only a **guide** to prices. A price range has been given for kitchenware items to allow for some wear and a little roughness that is normally not allowed in collecting other forms of Depression Glass. You will note that the price range has been widened in several areas, but particularly in reamer and measuring cup collecting. I have received pricing ideas from several dealers and collectors and the range of pricing was enough to stagger my mind. Since I, ultimately, must take the brunt of pricing discrepancies from collectors and dealers alike, I want you to know that the only rule in pricing seems to be determined by who owns it and who wishes to own it. In other words, only **two** people determine price, the buyer and the seller. **You**, ultimately, have to decide if the price is right for you.

The roughness or usage marks found on Kitchenware is a turn-off to some collectors who search for perfection. Remember, these were **utilitarian** items and were in **use** for years; therefore, most collectors will allow some roughness. This does not mean cracks, chips or chunks are acceptable. To the contrary, these greatly reduce the value of a piece. It simply means that kitchenware collectors are a little more lenient about the condition of the glassware than are collectors of Depression dinnerware. They have to be because **most of the kitchenware does not exist in absolutely mint condition!**

I have seen both higher and lower prices for most items shown; however, the prices listed are prices that collectors somewhere in the country have been willing to pay.

Colors

Any time the word green or pink occurs, it means a transparent (see-through) color. Other color items are described below.

Amethyst – a transparent, violet color.

Black Amethyst – color appears black but will show purple under a strong light.

Blue – "Chalaine," an opaque, sky blue made by McKee; "Cobalt," a transparent, dark blue; "Delphite," an opaque, medium blue made by Jeannette.

Clambroth – translucent off white or translucent green.

Custard – an opaque beige.

Green – "Jad-ite," an opaque green made by Hocking; "Jadite," an opaque green made by Jeannette; "Skokie," an opaque green made by McKee.

White – milk white; milk glass; opal white (all these terms simply indicate a white color); "Vitrock," a white made by Hocking.

Yellow– vaseline, a transparent greenish-yellow; "Seville" yellow, an opaque yellow made by McKee.

Contents

Part 1 – Colors
AMBER (Dark)

This book is divided into three sections: **Color**, **Items**, and **Patterns**, in that order. Thus, some items are pictured more than once. Hopefully, the prices are the same in each case of a repeated item. (I spent days trying to make certain of that.) However, feel free to report any discrepancies you find.

There are hundreds of new things shown in this book with the added pages; but to make room for them, some objects previously shown had to be omitted. I assume that you would prefer to see new items rather than different displays of things seen in earlier editions. However, for anyone discovering Depression era Kitchenware for the first time, we've still included all the basics.

At present, amber is not an avidly sought color, even though many pieces in it are rare. Reamer, measuring cup, and knife collectors are having difficulty finding amber pieces for their collections. Most Fry collectors would love to have the reamer shown in Row 4 or the meat platter in Row 5. By the same standard, various knife collectors are searching for the "Stonex" knife shown in Row 5.

So, keep in mind that not everyone collects Kitchenware by color. Many collectors seek only certain items. Therefore, the competition is intensified between these separate collecting fields.

Row	#	Item	Price
Row 1:	#1	Embossed "Coffee" canister	85.00– 95.00
	#2	Embossed "Tea" canister	70.00– 75.00
	#3-6	Spice shakers, ea.	20.00– 22.50
	#7	Salt box	150.00–165.00
	#8	Measuring cup	275.00–300.00
Row 2:	#1	Sugar canister	110.00–125.00
	#2	New Martinsville batter set	150.00–175.00
	#3	Cambridge etched grapes design ice bucket	35.00– 40.00
	#4	Valencia reamer, unembossed	250.00–300.00
Row 3:	#1	Water bottle	55.00– 65.00
	#2-5	U.S. Glass mixing bowl set (4)	80.00–100.00
		9" bowl	30.00– 35.00
		8" bowl	20.00– 25.00
		7" bowl	17.50– 22.50
		6" bowl	15.00– 17.50
Row 4:	#1	Cake stand (fairly recent vintage)	15.00– 17.50
	#2	Fry reamer	300.00–325.00
	#3	Butter dish (foreign)	40.00– 50.00
	#4	Butter dish (similar to canisters above)	50.00– 60.00
Row 5:	#1	Indiana Glass reamer	300.00–325.00
	#2	Fry meat platter	75.00– 85.00
	#3	Knife, 8¼", "Stonex"	175.00–195.00
	#4	Knife rest	17.50– 20.00
	#5	Apothecary measure, 1 oz.	25.00– 30.00

AMBER (Continued)

For some reason intense collectors of amber buy the darker shades; however, to have a usable set, you need to observe that amber color tints vary greatly as is portrayed by our pictures. Gathering only one shade of amber would be nearly impossible.

One note regarding the drawer pulls on Row 5. Drawer pulls with small screws are still more in demand than those with large screws ostensibly because smaller screws do not damage furniture as badly. However, you need to know that these are now being reproduced in many different colors. What I have seen are good copies, but the prices have been on a par with the prices of older ones, which is unfortunate.

Row 1:	#1	Chesterfield pitcher	90.00– 95.00
	#2	Chesterfield mug	22.50– 25.00
	#3	Imperial syrup	65.00– 75.00
	#4	Sugar shaker	250.00–275.00
	#5	"Visible" mail box	75.00– 85.00
Row 2:	#1	Cambridge oval covered casserole	50.00– 55.00
	#2	Cambridge covered casserole with underliner	40.00– 45.00
	#3	Cheese dish (possibly foreign)	65.00– 75.00
Row 3:	#1	U.S. Glass 2 cup and reamer top	300.00–325.00
	#2	Cambridge 2-spouted gravy boat	30.00– 35.00
	#3	Cambridge footed cream sauce boat for asparagus platter	30.00– 35.00
	#4	Westmoreland 2-piece reamer	175.00–200.00
	#5	Lemon reamer (foreign)	110.00–125.00
	#6	Oil bottle	30.00– 35.00
Row 4:	#1	Paden City "Party Line" ice bucket	27.50– 30.00
	#2	Same, 14 oz. tumbler	8.00– 10.00
	#3	Paden City egg cup	8.00– 10.00
	#4	Paden City hotel sugar and cover	20.00– 25.00
	#5	Paden City salt box	65.00– 75.00
	#6	Cambridge oil bottle	50.00– 55.00
	#7	Tobacco jar	30.00– 35.00
Row 5:	#1	"Feathered" curtain tie backs, pr.	22.50– 25.00
	#2	"Sandwich" round tie backs, pr.	20.00– 25.00
	#3	"Plume" tie backs or small round, pr.	17.50– 20.00
	#4	et. al. drawer pulls, ea. (large screws)	10.00– 12.50
		Same w/small screws	10.00– 12.50
	#5	Door knobs, set	85.00– 95.00

AMBER and BLACK (Milk glass or amethyst)

The shade of amber most easily found is the lighter shade shown in lower half of the photo on page 11. There is a reluctance on the part of present day collectors to buy amber as a kitchen collectible; and because of this, there have been some price corrections in this book. (That is a polite way of saying some prices have dropped!) Reamers, sugar shakers, and unusual items are still in demand, but common pieces remain difficult to sell. The Cambridge reamer (Row 3, #1) is one of the prime amber collectibles; however, even it is not as easily sold as it was a few years ago! Measuring cups (Row 4, #3 and Row 5, #3) are examples of supply equaling demand.

Black still carries a mystique all its own for collectors. Have you noticed how many modern kitchens are using black as a decorating color? Our home in Florida has a major black color scheme in the kitchen appliances. All five reamers shown on page 13 are prizes worthy of possessing, but they can annihilate the glass budget.

Amber
Page 11

Row 1:	#1	Cocktail shaker	100.00–110.00
	#2-4	Jars (recent vintage)	15.00– 20.00
	#5	Tobacco jar	30.00– 35.00
	#6	Sugar shaker	100.00–110.00
Row 2:	#1	Batter jug, Paden City	50.00– 60.00
	#2	Tobacco jar	18.00– 20.00
	#3	Sugar shaker, Paden City	200.00–225.00
	#4	Sugar shaker	200.00–250.00
	#5	Sugar shaker	150.00–200.00
	#6	Syrup, Cambridge	60.00– 65.00
Row 3:	#1	Reamer, Cambridge	600.00–700.00
	#2	Reamer, foreign	75.00– 85.00
	#3	Reamer, top only	50.00– 60.00
		Same, complete	150.00–175.00

Row 3: (Continued)			
	#4	Sugar Shaker, Paden City	200.00– 225.00
	#5	Syrup	45.00– 55.00
Row 4:	#1	Reamer, Westmoreland	250.00–300.00
	#2	Butter, 1/4 lb., Federal	25.00– 30.00
	#3	Measure cup, no handle	35.00– 37.50
	#4	Butter, 1/4 lb., Federal	25.00– 30.00
	#5	Jelly jar	12.00– 15.00
Row 5:	**All Federal Glass Company**		
	#1	Butter, 1 lb.	30.00– 35.00
	#2	Butter tub	30.00– 35.00
	#3	Measure cup, w/handle	35.00– 38.00
	#4	Reamer, tab handle	15.00– 20.00
	#5	Reamer, tab handle	275.00–300.00

Black
Page 12

Row 1:	#1	Cookie jar, L. E. Smith	75.00– 85.00
	#2	Batter jug, Fenton	150.00– 175.00
	#3	Syrup, same	100.00– 125.00
	#4	Reamer pitcher, Fenton	1,200.00–1,400.00
Row 2:	#1	Ice bucket	60.00– 65.00
	#2	Jar, import?	15.00– 20.00
	#3	Sugar shaker	325.00– 375.00
	#4	Saunders reamer	1,250.00–1,400.00
Row 3:	#1	McKee grapefruit reamer	1,100.00–1,200.00
	#2	Sunkist reamer	700.00– 750.00
	#3-5	Shakers, ea.	25.00– 30.00
	#6	Tray for batter set	30.00– 35.00

Row 4:	#1	Mixing bowl, 9 3/8"	60.00– 65.00
		Bowl, 8 3/8" (not shown)	50.00– 55.00
		Bowl, 7 3/8" (not shown)	50.00– 55.00
		Bowl, 6 3/8" (not shown)	40.00– 45.00
		Bowl, 5 3/8" (not shown)	40.00– 45.00
	#2	Bowl, 7 3/8" McKee	30.00– 40.00
	#3	Mug	22.00– 25.00
	#4	Ladle	25.00– 30.00
Row 5:	#1	McKee, 2 spout	800.00– 900.00
	#2	Reamer, Tricia	1,400.00–1,500.00
	#3	Tray	25.00– 30.00
	#4	Shaker, Fenton hobnail	25.00– 30.00

Page 13

Row 1:	#1	Sellers sugar canister	90.00–110.00
	#2	Salt or pepper, ea.	20.00– 25.00
	#3	McKee batter jug	120.00–140.00
	#4	Cocktail shaker	60.00– 75.00
	#5	Syrup, covered, Fenton	100.00–125.00
Row 2:	#1	McKee, 4 1/2" salt (harder to find than pepper)	25.00– 30.00
		Same, pepper (weak lettering–50% of prices)	20.00– 25.00
		Same, flour or sugar	40.00– 45.00
	#2	McKee, 3 1/2" sugar (priced as above)	40.00– 45.00
	#3	Covered ice bucket	75.00– 85.00
	#4	McKee tumbler	15.00– 18.00
	#5	Straw in tumbler	8.00– 10.00
	#6	Paden City batter jug set	275.00–295.00

Row 3:		All shakers priced as in Row 2 (with those having badly worn or missing lettering 50% of prices listed) EXCEPT last pr.	35.00– 40.00
Row 4:	#1	Butter dish w/crystal top (possibly foreign)	85.00– 95.00
	#2	Egg cup	16.00– 18.00
	#3	Drawer pull, double	20.00– 25.00
	#4	Paden City, "Party Line" napkin holder	135.00–150.00
	#5	Nar-O-Fold Napkin Company Chicago, U.S.A.	135.00–150.00
Row 5:	#1	Punch ladle	100.00–125.00
	#2-5	Drawer pulls, ea.	16.00– 18.00
	#3	Cambridge salad set	125.00–150.00

BLUE (Chalaine) and PEACOCK BLUE

Chalaine blue is one of the more challenging colors to find in Depression Kitchenware. It is often confused with Delphite blue by beginning collectors. I have always referred to Chalaine as "robin's egg" blue to help distinguish the color from Delphite.

Cathy and I decided to break up the set we were collecting when we moved ... again! Color schemes were vastly different! We made several collectors very happy! Our canisters went to a lady who has since confessed to having a baker's dozen of them!

Several of the costly rolling pins have surfaced lately. Besides the rolling pin, the measuring pitcher without a handle is the most elusive piece. Only two of these have been found and the price is notably high on these. Good strong lettering on the shakers and canisters is necessary; but beware that there are "artists" who have been known to "doctor" this black lettering.

Peacock Blue now seems to be as plentiful as Chalaine, but neither color is abundant. You should find Peacock blue canisters with serious searching. Labeling is not a problem with this color since the names are embossed in the glass.

Chalaine Blue

Page 15

Row	#	Item	Price
Row 1:	#1	Vase, 12"	100.00– 125.00
	#2	Measure pitcher, 4 cup, without handle	1,250.00–1,500.00
	#3	Measure pitcher, 4 cup, ftd.	400.00– 450.00
	#4	Pitcher, ftd. (possibly Fenton)	200.00– 250.00
Row 2:	#1-6	Shakers, ea.	90.00– 95.00
	#7,8	Shakers, embossed	125.00– 150.00
	#9	Measure cup, 2 spout	800.00– 900.00
Row 3:	#1	Refrigerator dish, 7¼" sq.	110.00–125.00
	#2	Refrigerator dish, 4" x 5"	40.00– 50.00
	#3	Canister, rnd., 10 oz., blue lid	40.00– 55.00
	#4	Canister, rnd., 24 oz., blue lid	40.00– 55.00
	#5	Canister, rnd., 48 oz., blue lid	65.00– 85.00
Row 4:	#1-4	Canisters (press-on lids), ea.	400.00–425.00
	#5	Sunkist reamer	200.00–225.00

Page 16

Row	#	Item	Price
Row 1:	#1	Ladle, screw on handle	175.00– 200.00
	#2	Rolling pin, shaker top	1,500.00–1,800.00
Row 2:	#1	Beater bowl, w/spout, 4" tall	75.00– 85.00
	#2,5	Drawer pull, single	16.00– 18.00
	#3	Butter dish, ribbed, tab handles	325.00– 375.00
	#4	Fruit jar	75.00– 100.00
	#6	Egg cup	15.00– 18.00
Row 2: (Continued)	#7	Small jar	17.50– 20.00
Row 3:	#1	Mixing bowl, 9¼"	110.00–125.00
	#2	Same, 7½"	85.00– 95.00
	#3	Same, 6"	85.00– 95.00
	#4	Door knob	75.00– 85.00
Row 4:	#1	Mixing bowl, 9"	110.00–125.00
	#2	Mixing bowl, 9", ribbed	110.00–125.00
	#3	Flower pot, Akro Agate	20.00– 25.00

Peacock Blue

Page 17

Row	#	Item	Price
Row 1:	#1	Strawholder (probably 1950's)	100.00– 150.00
	#2	L.E. Smith cookie jar	75.00– 100.00
	#3	Imperial decanter	35.00– 45.00
	#4	Dispenser (for a liquid or syrup)	200.00– 250.00
Row 2:	#1	Sugar, 5 lb. canister	300.00– 325.00
	#2	Coffee, 40 oz. canister	175.00– 195.00
	#3	Tea, 20 oz. canister	175.00– 195.00
	#4-6	Shakers, 8 oz., ea.	50.00– 55.00
	#7	Salt box	125.00– 150.00
Row 3:	#1	Ice tub	35.00– 40.00
	#2	Rolling pin	250.00– 275.00
Row 3: (Continued)	#3	Mug	25.00–30.00
Row 4:	#1	Jar (paper label, sold by route merchants)	15.00–17.50
	#2-8	Tie backs, large pr.	25.00–30.00
		small pr.	20.00–25.00
Row 5:	#1	Towel rod	40.00–45.00
	#2	Double towel rod	40.00–45.00
	#3	Towel rod	30.00–35.00
Row 6:	#1, 2	Spoons, ea.	22.50–25.00
	#3, 4	Salad set	55.00–70.00
	#5, 6	Double drawer pulls, ea.	20.00–25.00
	#7-11	Single drawer pulls, ea.	15.00–18.00

17

BLUE (Cobalt)

A word of warning to those of you who may have found a cobalt blue rolling pin recently. An "old" cobalt blue rolling pin with a screw-on metal cap was never found. In fact, no rolling pins with screw-on metal lids have ever been found in a transparent color other than crystal. I mention that here because I am receiving letters regularly about these "rare" finds. I'm sorry, but they are all newly made.

The mystique of the cobalt blue color continues. Some collectors recently have been willing to pay "whatever it takes" to finish up their collections. Unfortunately, that makes it difficult to fairly price some rarely found items that have sold recently. Just because a wealthy collector buys an item at a big price does not necessarily mean the next like item on the market will fetch a big price also. Cobalt blue canisters with exceptional lettering and undamaged lids are bringing phenomonal prices. There are a few canisters with worn lettering and chipped lids available, but collectors are willing to pay a premium for mint canisters. Know that lettering is sometimes being redone on worn canisters!

Items with an asterisk (*) in the book have been reproduced! See pages 236-237 for further information. On page 19, Row 2, #1 and #5 have both been reproduced and the price made a downward adjustment for a while. It was only temporary!

Page 19   All Hazel Atlas except last row.

Row 1: #1-5 Canister w/lid (deduct 75.00-100.00 for worn lettering) 375.00–425.00

Row 2:
#1 2-Cup measure w/reamer top *275.00–295.00
#2 Tab-handled orange reamer 275.00–295.00
#3 Tab-handled lemon reamer 300.00–325.00
#4 Milk pitcher 85.00–100.00
#5 1-Cup measure, 3 spout *350.00–400.00

Row 3:
#1 Stack refrigerator, 4½" x 5", ea. 40.00– 45.00
#2 Round refrigerator, 5³/4" 60.00– 75.00
#3 Water bottle, 64 oz., 10" tall 55.00– 60.00

Row 3: (Continued)
#4 Hazel Atlas bottle, (possibly medicinal) 20.00– 25.00
#5 Mixer, Vidrio Products 110.00–125.00

Row 4:
#1 Butter dish 225.00–250.00
#2 Bowl, 5³/4", "Restwell" 25.00– 30.00
#3 Bowl, 6" 25.00– 30.00
#4 Tumbler, marked HA 15.00– 18.00

Row 5:
#1 Spoon stirrer 12.50– 15.00
#2 Curtain tie back 15.00– 17.50
#3 Drawer pull 16.00– 18.00
#4, 5 Stirrers, ea. 1.50– 2.50
#6-8 Spoons or forks, ea. 27.50– 35.00
#9 Coaster 5.00– 7.50

Page 20

Row 1:
#1 Bowl, 8½" (add $5.00 w/metal) 35.00–40.00
#2 Bowl, 7⁵/8" (add $5.00 w/metal) 30.00–35.00
#3 Bowl, 6⁵/8" (add $5.00 w/metal) 30.00–35.00

Row 2:
#1 Bowl, 9⁵/8" (add $5.00 w/metal) 45.00–50.00
#2 Bowl, 11⁵/8" 70.00–75.00
#3 Bowl, 10⁵/8" (all of above are Hazel Atlas) 85.00–95.00

Row 3:
#1 L.E. Smith water dispenser 400.00–450.00
#2 Cambridge mug 35.00– 50.00
#3 Shakers, pr. (possibly bath powder) 20.00– 25.00

Row 4:
#1 L.E. Smith bowl, 8¼" 50.00– 55.00
#2 Same, 7¼" 45.00– 50.00
#3 Same, 6¼" 40.00– 45.00

Row 5:
#1 Mustard pot 25.00– 30.00
#2 Fry cake plate, 3 ftd. 110.00–125.00
#3, 4 Fork and spoon, set 50.00– 55.00

Page 21

Row 1:
#1 Barbell cocktail shaker 85.00– 95.00
#2 Strawholder 250.00–275.00
#3 Cocktail shaker 60.00– 65.00
#4 McKee batter jug 95.00–125.00

Row 2:
#1 New Martinsville batter set 375.00–395.00
#2, 3 Shakers w/blue tops 50.00– 55.00
#4 Sugar shaker (older than Depression era) 225.00–250.00
#5 Sugar shaker 900.00–950.00

Row 2: (Continued)
#6 Tumble up 80.00– 85.00

Row 3:
#1 Paden City batter jug 90.00– 95.00
#2 Same, milk jug 90.00– 95.00
#3 Same, syrup jug 90.00– 95.00
#4 Cambridge reamer 2,000.00–2,500.00

Row 4:
#1 Cobalt rolling pin 400.00– 450.00
#2 Cobalt handles rolling pin 250.00– 300.00

BLUE (Delphite), Jeannette Glass Co., Late '30's

"Usually a color that is featured on the cover may experience some price escalation. So be forewarned!" With those words I closed my comments on Delphite in the fourth edition. What a prophecy!

After that cover appearance, dealers could not find enough Delphite to satisfy collectors' demands. With a limited amount of pieces being offered for sale, prices on Jeannette's Delphite began to skyrocket and you can see the results in the listings below. Delphite remains one of the most alluring colors of Kitchen collectibles.

Jeannette round canisters are becoming impossible to find at *any* price. The coffee canister remains the easiest of the larger canisters to find, while many collectors have never happened upon the sugar. You may find the smaller round shakers, especially the salt and pepper, but the flour, sugar, and paprika are all elusive. Next to the square shakers in Row 4 is a one-cup measure without a spout. Someone has ground off a badly chipped spout!

The larger-size Delphite reamer is depicted in Row 3, #1 with the more commonly found smaller reamer beside it for comparison. All drippings jars are not found with black lettering. The price without the lettering is only half (or less) of the price shown below. Watch out for repainted letters on these.

I wish you luck in your search for this color.

Row 1:	#1	Canister, 40 oz., sugar	350.00– 375.00
	#2	Same, coffee	350.00– 375.00
	#3	Canister, 20 oz., tea	145.00– 155.00
	#4	Shaker, 8 oz., paprika	105.00– 115.00
	#5	Same, sugar	100.00– 120.00
		Same, flour (not shown)	100.00– 120.00
	#6	Matches holder	85.00– 95.00
	#7	Bowl w/metal beater	60.00– 70.00
Row 2:	#1	Bowl, 5½", horizontal rib	60.00– 65.00
	#2	Measure, 1 cup	50.00– 55.00
		Same, ½ cup	45.00– 50.00
		Same, ⅓ cup	40.00– 50.00
		Same, ¼ cup	35.00– 40.00
		set	170.00– 195.00
	#3	Bowl, 7½", horizontal rib	60.00– 75.00
	#4	Bowl, 9¾", horizontal rib	80.00– 95.00
		Bowl set #1, 3, 4 set	200.00– 235.00
Row 3:	#1	Reamer, large	1,000.00–1,250.00
	#2	Reamer, small	75.00– 95.00
	#3	Shaker, salt	45.00– 50.00
	#5	Shaker, pepper	40.00– 45.00
	#4	Drippings jar w/lettering	110.00– 125.00
Row 4:	#1	2-cup pitcher sunflower bottom	70.00– 75.00
	#2	Butter	250.00– 285.00
	#3	Cup measure (spout professionally removed)	25.00– 30.00
	#4, 5	Shaker, square salt or pepper	75.00– 85.00
	#6, 7	Same, flour or sugar	85.00– 95.00
Row 5:	#1-3	Canister, square, 29 oz., 5", ea.	175.00– 195.00
	#4, 5	Mixing bowl set (4) vertical rib	220.00– 260.00
		Bowl, 6", rare	75.00– 95.00
		Bowl, 7"	55.00– 65.00
		Bowl, 8"	55.00– 65.00
		Bowl, 9"	85.00– 95.00

BLUE (Delphite) and BLUE MISCELLANEOUS

The reamer top shown below is atop most Delphite and reamer collectors' want lists. In the center is the only known McKee screw-lid canister. There are surely more somewhere!

As with Jeannette's Delphite, there is not enough McKee Delphite found to satisfy the demand.

Page 24

	#1	Reamer pitcher	1,250.00–1,500.00
	#2	Canister, 48 oz.	200.00– 250.00
	#3	Electric beater	85.00– 95.00

Page 25

Row 1:	#1	McKee measure pitcher, 4 cup	500.00– 550.00
	#2	McKee measure pitcher, 2 cup	75.00– 85.00
	#3	McKee 48 oz. round canister	120.00– 135.00
	#4	McKee 10 oz. round canister	40.00– 45.00
	#5	Vase	30.00– 35.00
	#6	Ginger (?) jar	15.00– 18.00

Row 2:	#1	McKee butter dish	250.00– 285.00
	#2	McKee refrigerator dish, 4" x 5"	27.50– 30.00
	#3, 4	Shakers, ea.	85.00– 95.00
	#5	Ash tray, possibly McKee or Pyrex	12.00– 15.00

Row 3:	#1	Mixing bowl, 9"	85.00– 95.00
	#2	Mixing bowl, 7³/₈"	50.00– 55.00
	#3	Bowl w/spout, 4¹/₄"	65.00– 75.00
	#4	Bowl, 4³/₈" (cocotte)	18.00– 20.00

Row 4:	#1	L.E. Smith, 9¹/₄" bowl	60.00– 75.00
	#2	L.E. Smith, 7" bowl	40.00– 50.00
	#3	Fry, cornflower blue reamer	1,500.00–1,750.00
	#4	Hocking, "Block Optic" butter dish	375.00– 425.00

Row 5:	#1	Cheese dish (possibly foreign)	100.00– 110.00
	#2	Scoop	55.00– 65.00
	#3	Paden City bunny, cotton ball dispenser	125.00– 150.00
	#4	Soap dish, "Home Soap Company"	22.50– 25.00

"CLAMBROTH" WHITE and CRYSTAL

The translucent, washed-out white color shown in the bottom three rows on page 27 is commonly called "Clambroth" (white) by collectors. Although this is a rarely found color (except for the rolling pin), there is not much collector demand for "Clambroth" white either. A remarkable exception to that statement is the oval Pyrex casserole pictured in the middle of Row 3. This casserole is embossed "Pyrex" on one end and "193-197" on the other. Only one of these has appeared so far. You can see additional pieces of "Clambroth" white in the reamer section.

Collectors of crystal kitchenware still have fair prices at their disposal when compared to prices of other popular colored wares. However, be warned that the acquisition of crystal is beginning to deplete even this supply. Many older items can be found at prices comparable to recently manufactured wares.

On page 29, Row 4 #1 is an item marked, "The Pot Watcher." My understanding is that this is placed in the bottom of a pan or pot, and when the pot begins to boil, this glass piece begins to rattle around announcing that the pot is boiling. Another collector wrote that placing this in the bottom would cause the water to not boil over. (These are presently available in hardware stores.)

Page 27

Row 1:	#1	Canister, Owens-Illinois, frosted, 40 oz.	18.00– 20.00
	#2, 3	Same, 20 oz.	16.00– 18.00
	#4, 5	Cruet, frosted, chicken decal, ea.	12.00– 15.00
Row 2:	#1	Rolling pin w/wooden handles	125.00–150.00
	#2	Sugar shaker, lid w/one hole	40.00– 45.00
	#3, 4	Salt or pepper w/normal lid	15.00– 17.50

Row 3:	#1	Canister, large	30.00– 35.00
	#2	Pyrex oval casserole	100.00–125.00
	#3	Canister, medium	25.00– 30.00
		wo/label subtract $5.00 on canisters	
Row 4:	#1	Tray, 10⅝", square	12.00– 15.00
	#2	Server, 7⅜", round	10.00– 12.00
	#3	Server, 9⅞", round	12.00– 15.00

Page 28

Row 1:	#1	Canister, large, w/"Taverne" scene	30.00–35.00
	#2	Canister, medium, same (rare size)	40.00–45.00
	#3, 4	Shaker, ovoid shape, Owens–Illinois, ea.	10.00–12.50
	#5	Canister, ovoid shape, Owens-Illinois	20.00–25.00
Row 2:	#1	Instant coffee, w/sterling top	25.00–30.00
	#2	"Bohner's Safety crushed fruit bowl" (pat. Feb 22, 1898)	20.00–25.00

Row 2:	(Continued)		
	#3-7	Sneath spice shaker, ea	10.00–12.50
Row 3:	#1	Fleur-de-lis flour canister	20.00–22.50
	#2-4	Canister, 20 oz. ea.	10.00–12.00
	#5	8 oz. Kroger Embassy peanut butter	8.00–10.00
	#6	Spee-Dee mixer	20.00–25.00
Row 4:	#1-6	Small canister, 16 oz., ea.	7.00– 8.00
	#7	MOXIE (licensed only for serving)	20.00–25.00

Page 29

Row 1:	#1	Canister, Dutch boy design	15.00–20.00
	#2	Canister, embossed coffee	20.00–25.00
	#3	Canister, emb. coffee, Zipper design	20.00–25.00
	#4	"Kwik Whip all purpose mixer"	6.00– 8.00
	#5	"No Drip Server," Federal Tool Corp., 1 qt.	12.00–15.00
Row 2:	#1	Salt, large	20.00–25.00
	#2	Salt, small	20.00–22.50
	#3	Canister, embossed tea	18.00–20.00
	#4	Syrup, w/glass top (2 pc.)	25.00–30.00
	#5	Pint server (same as #5 in Row 1)	12.00–15.00

Row 3:	#1, 6	Glasbake tea kettle, ea.	30.00–35.00
	#2	Canister, raised dots design	15.00–18.00
	#3-5	Shaker, raised dot design, ea.	4.00– 5.00
Row 4:	#1	"The Pot Watcher"	8.00–10.00
	#2	McKee Range Tec skillet	9.00–10.00
	#3-8	Six-piece set from box marked "Serve U Set" Medco No 86:	
		Salt and Pepper, pair	4.00
		Syrup	15.00–17.50
		Ketchup	15.00–17.50
		Marmalade	8.00–10.00
		Sugar	18.00–20.00

CRYSTAL

Crystal kitchenware lends itself to any kitchen decor and has the added attraction of see-through storage. Prices remain reasonable on most items. Unlike many of today's products that are made to be disposed of after one use, it can be used over and over. The McKee water dispenser shown below has a separate center holder for the ice. I guess that idea never caught on, but it seems like a neat idea to me! The cooler below sells for $85.00–100.00. It is that insert for the ice that can seldom be found.

Row 1:	#1	McKee Glasbake Scientific Measuring Cup	20.00–25.00
	#2-5	Hocking canister w/Dutch decal	15.00–20.00
	#6	Pint measure in tablespoons for coffee, tea & wine	18.00–20.00
Row 2:	#1, 2	John Alden (salt) & Priscilla (pepper), pr.	17.50–20.00
	#3	Westmoreland baby reamer, w/decal	35.00–40.00
	#4	Horseradish jar	10.00–12.50
	#5	Salt box	15.00–17.50
	#6	Toast holder	50.00–65.00
	#7	Spoon holder (Pat. Feb. 11, 1913)	20.00–22.00
Row 3:	#1-8	Dutch shakers (12 oz.), ea. (Cocoa in 6th)	8.00– 9.00
	#9-10	Dutch shakers (16 oz.)	10.00–12.00
Row 4:	#1	Flour canister, 128 oz.	40.00–45.00
	#2	Coffee dripolator	20.00–25.00
	#3	Measure spoon (markings for table, dessert, tea)	12.00–15.00
	#4	Sprinkler (leaning in back) cardboard wrapped instructions	20.00–25.00
	#5	Cambridge ash tray holder	30.00–35.00
	#6	Jiffy one-cup coffee maker w/filter	8.00–10.00

CUSTARD and "CARAMEL," McKee Glass Company

The darker shade of Custard (shown in the bottom row on page 33), is referred to as "caramel" by collectors. This color may have been experimental or just a bad batch of Custard. Today, we do not have the luxury of obtaining that information. The canister on the far right is not a fired-on color, but a solid, caramel color like the other pieces. I mention that because I have seen a few fired-on pieces similar in color.

There are some avid collectors of the Custard colored ware, but its popularity with most collectors is still lackluster. Many pieces are commonly found, but some are elusive. Although the Sunkist custard reamer is abundant, custard grapefruit reamers are rare.

If you would like a challenge, try putting together a set of four (salt, pepper, flour, sugar) in any particular lettering design. Unless you are lucky enough to buy a complete set at one time, it will take a lot of searching to come up with a matching set.

Page 33

Row 1:	#1, 2	Canister, coffee or tea, ea.	35.00– 40.00
	#3	Measure pitcher, 4 cup	30.00– 35.00
	#4	Bowl, 9"	18.00– 20.00
Row 2:	#1	Bowl, 8"	15.00– 18.00
		Bowl, 7" (not shown)	12.00– 15.00
	#2	Bowl, 6"	10.00– 12.00
	#3, 4	Shaker, Roman arch, flour, sugar	18.00– 20.00
	#5, 6	Same, salt or pepper	12.00– 15.00
Row 3:	#1-4	Salt or pepper shakers, ea.	10.00– 12.00
	#5	Cinnamon shaker	25.00– 30.00
	#6-9	Flour or sugar shaker, ea.	17.50– 20.00
Row 4:	#1	Pepper shaker	12.50– 15.00
	#2	Lady w/apron shaker	17.50– 20.00
	#3	Custard or jello	8.00– 10.00
	#4	Pitcher, 2 cup	20.00– 22.00
	#5	Tumbler	8.00– 10.00
	#6	Tom & Jerry mug	12.00– 15.00
Row 5:	#1	Reamer, 6" embossed McK	30.00– 35.00
	#2	Grapefruit reamer	600.00–650.00
	#3	Sunkist reamer	35.00– 38.00
Row 6:	**All Caramel Color**		
	#1	Canister, 40 oz.	65.00– 75.00
	#2	Grapefruit reamer	750.00–850.00
	#3	Sunkist reamer	350.00–385.00
	#4	Measure cup, 2 spout	500.00–600.00
	#5	Canister, 48 oz	85.00–100.00

EMERALD-GLO, FOREST GREEN AND GREEN "CLAM-BROTH"

The items pictured on page 35 have been found labeled "Cavalier Emerald-Glo Hand-Made." You will find additional pieces to this set; let me hear what you find! Most pieces are cut with a star. Those with a star cut were made by Paden City. Pieces without a star cut were made by both Paden City and Fenton. Fenton's pieces are a darker green shade when set side by side with those of Paden City. All Emerald-Glo was made for Rubel.

Emerald-Glo
Page 35

Row 1:	#1	Sugar w/liner	20.00–22.00
	#2	Condiment set	30.00–35.00
	#3	Marmalade w/spoon	20.00–25.00
Row 2:	#1	Handled relish	25.00–30.00
	#2	Salad bowl w/fork and spoon	50.00–55.00
	#3	Individual creamer/sugar on tray	22.50–25.00

Row 3:	#1	Covered casserole	30.00–35.00
	#2	Mayonnaise w/spoon	20.00–25.00
	#3	Syrup w/liner	30.00–35.00
Row 4:	#1	Handled server	40.00–50.00
	#2	Handled cheese dish	40.00–50.00

Forest Green
Page 36

Row 1:	#1	Owens-Illinois vinegar or water bottle w/tray	30.00–35.00
		Same w/o tray	15.00–20.00
	#2	Hocking water bottle w/top	25.00–30.00
	#3	Duraglas water bottle	20.00–25.00
	#4	McKee syrup (goes with #5)	30.00–35.00
	#5	Oil & Vinegar set (goes w/#4)	30.00–35.00
Row 2:	#1, 2	Owens-Illinois canisters (ovoid shape), ea.	50.00–55.00
		Same, medium size TEA, RICE (not shown)	40.00–50.00
	#3	Same, shaker size	15.00–17.50
		Prices for #1, 2, 3 (30% to 40% less w/missing lettering)	
	#4	Owens-Illinois embossed COFFEE w/flip top	50.00–65.00

Row 2:	(Continued)		
	#5	Owens-Illinois water bottle	12.50– 15.00
Row 3:	#1-3	Owens-Illinois 40 oz. diagonal ridged canister, ea.	25.00– 30.00
	#4-5	Same, 20 oz., ea (TEA, RICE)	25.00– 30.00
	#6	Same, 10 oz.	15.00– 17.50
	#7, 8	Shakers, ea.	3.00– 4.00
Row 4:	#1	New Martinsville batter jug	75.00– 85.00
	#2	Same, syrup jug	65.00– 85.00
	#3	Cruet	35.00– 40.00
	#4	Sugar shaker (1950's)	75.00– 85.00
Row 5:	#1, 2	Curtain rings, ea.	10.00– 12.50
	#3	Rolling pin	125.00–150.00
	#4, 5	Shakers, pr.	17.50– 20.00

Green "Clambroth" etc.
Page 37

Row 1:	#1-4	Hocking canisters w/glass lid, 47 oz., ea.	50.00– 55.00
	#5-8	Hocking shakers, 8 oz. ea.	17.50– 20.00
Row 2:	#1	Hocking oval refrig. dish, 8"	30.00– 35.00
	#2	Same, 7"	25.00– 30.00
	#3	Same, 6"	20.00– 25.00
	#4	Refrigerator jar, 4 1/4" x 4 3/4"	25.00– 27.50
	#5	Hocking drippings jar (possibly powder jar)	35.00– 40.00
	#6	Hocking 2-cup measure	125.00–150.00
Row 3:	#1	Hocking 1-cup measure	200.00–225.00
	#2	Hocking reamer	150.00–175.00
	#3	Fenton reamer top for pitcher	65.00– 75.00
	#4	Jadite Sunkist (there is one that is much more translucent than this)	30.00– 35.00

Row 3:	(Continued)		
	#5	Cold cream jar	20.00– 22.00
	#6	Mug	30.00– 35.00
Row 4:	#1	Owl "tumble-up" nite set (pitcher & glass as top)	85.00–100.00
	#2	Butter dish	110.00–125.00
	#3	McKee Hall's refrigerator dish, 4" x 6"	18.00– 20.00
	#4	Water dispenser w/crystal top	110.00–125.00
Row 5:	#1	Ice bucket, Fenton	50.00– 55.00
	#2	Whipped cream pail	35.00– 40.00
	#3	Fenton pitcher missing lid (as pictured)	75.00– 85.00
	#4	Towel bar holders, pr.	20.00– 25.00
	#5	Sugar shaker	35.00– 40.00
	#6	"Serv-All" napkin holder	175.00–195.00

GREEN "CLAMBROTH" and JADITE

As with "Clambroth" white, the term "Clambroth" refers to a collector name for the translucent green pictured on pages 37 and 39. It is not a company name. Shown on pages 40 and 41 are a combination of different companies' Jadite. Hocking spelled their color Jad-ite. The only spouted Jadite measuring cup that I have heard about is shown at the top of page 40. On page 41 in Row 3 is a Jad-ite skillet with a label reading, "Yours with Gold Medal Flour; 1 w 25 lb. sack; 2 w 50 lb. sack; New Fire-King Oven Ware."

Page 39

Row 1:	#1	Pitcher (Fenton?)	60.00– 75.00
	#2	Tumbler to match above	12.00– 15.00
	#3	Fenton ice bucket & lid	110.00–125.00
	#4	Tumbler, ftd.	12.00– 15.00
	#5	Sherbet	12.00– 15.00
	#6	Door knob set	75.00– 95.00
Row 2:	#1	Mixing bowl, 8³/₄"	25.00– 30.00
	#2	Same, 7³/₄"	20.00– 25.00
	#3	Same, 6³/₄"	18.00– 20.00
	#4	Powder shaker?	22.50– 25.00
Row 3:	#1	Ashtray	5.00– 6.00
	#2	Wall tumbler holder	15.00– 18.00
	#3	Coaster	8.00– 10.00
	#4	Furniture "foot rest" (per 1920's Montgomery Ward catalogue)	4.00– 5.00
	#5	Jadite towel bar in rear	30.00– 35.00

Row 3: (Continued)			
	#6	Soap dish	17.50– 20.00
	#7	Jade ashtray	5.00– 8.00
	#8	Jade makeup holder	18.00– 20.00
Row 4:	#1, 2	Canisters, fired-on ea.	25.00– 30.00
	#3	Decanter, pinched	125.00–145.00
	#4	Water bottle	150.00–175.00
	#5	Bowl, 4³/₄" twist design	10.00– 12.00
	#6	McKee bottoms up w/coaster (coaster $90.00-100.00)	145.00–165.00
Row 5:	#1	Jadite vinegar cruet	250.00–275.00
	#2	Refrigerator dish, wedge shaped	15.00– 20.00
	#3	Refrigerator w/jade lid	10.00– 12.00
	#4	Cigarette ashtray	20.00– 22.00
	#5	Bowl, 4¹/₂"	10.00– 12.00

Page 40

Row 1:	#1	Spouted ¹/₂ cup measure	125.00–150.00
	#2	Jeannette souvenir shakers, pr.	100.00–125.00
Row 2:	#1	Fire-King miniature skillet	35.00– 40.00

	#2-5	Child's size 3" canister, ea. (don't confuse w/reg. 3" spice shakers, p. 43)	225.00–250.00
Row 3:	#1-4	Jeannette toiletry shakers, ea.	110.00–125.00

Page 41

Row 1:	#1	Hocking Jad-ite 7¹/₂" bowl (decorated)	15.00– 18.00
	#2	McKee embossed Salt	45.00– 50.00
	#3	McKee 4" x 5" drippings	75.00– 85.00
	#4	Jeannette Epsom Salt	110.00–125.00
	#5	Hocking Jad-ite 6¹/₂" bowl (decorated)	12.00– 15.00
Row 2:	#1	Hocking embossed Fire-King mug	45.00– 50.00
	#2	Hocking 7 oz. mug	5.00– 6.00
	#3	Hocking 16 oz. pitcher	15.00– 20.00
	#4	Hocking St. Denis cup	6.00– 8.00
	#5	Hocking 6 oz. straight cup	5.00– 6.00
Row 3:	#1	"Swedish Modern," "Jad-ite," 11" mixing bowl, 3 qt.	20.00–22.00

		Same, 9¹/₂", 2 qt. (not shown)	18.00–20.00
		Same, 8", 1 qt. (not shown)	15.00–18.00
	#2	Same, 6¹/₂", 1 pt.	12.00–15.00
	#3	Jad-ite ¹/₂ pound butter	20.00–25.00
	#4	Jad-ite one spout skillet	20.00–25.00
		Same w/label	25.00–30.00
Row 4:	#1	Leftover refrigerator jar	10.00–12.00
	#2,3	Plate, 9⁵/₈", 5 compartment	12.50–15.00
		Cup, 6 oz.	5.00– 6.00
	#4	Handiwhip w/beater	25.00–30.00
Row 5:	#1	Jad-ite Mixing bowl, 9"	15.00–18.00
	#2	Same, 8"	12.00–15.00
	#3	Same, 7"	10.00–12.00
	#4	Same, 6"	10.00–12.00

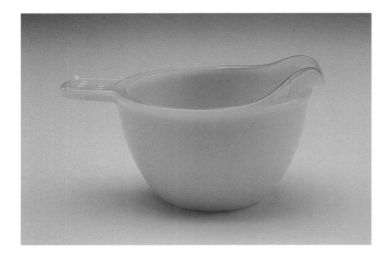

GREEN JADITE, Jeannette and McKee Companies, (Called "SKOKIE GREEN" by McKee)

Jadite continues to be very popular with collectors. Although there are some price discrepancies between dark and light colors of Jadite, there are still more collectors buying the lighter color. The price of many of the abundantly produced items remains equitable despite heavy demand. Other items, as can be seen by the price, are not so easily found. The batter jug shown in the bottom row can be found. It is the lid that is nigh impossible!

Page 43 (Jeannette Glass Co.)

Row 1:	#1-4	Canister, square, 5½" high, 48 oz., ea.	65.00–70.00
		Same, Floral pattern inside lid	65.00–70.00
	#5	Beater bowl, w/beater	25.00–30.00
Row 2:	#1, 2	Jadite, light, salt or pepper	15.00–17.50
#3, 4		Same, flour or sugar	22.50–25.00
	#5, 6	Jadite, dark, salt or pepper	15.00–17.50
	#7, 8	Same, flour or sugar	22.50–25.00
	#9	Butter, light	40.00–45.00
Row 3:	#1	Reamer, large, light	25.00–30.00
	#2	Same, dark	30.00–35.00
	#3	Refrigerator dish, 5" x 5" (Floral lid)	20.00–22.00
	#4	Butter, dark	45.00–50.00
Row 4:	#1-4	Canister, square, 29 oz., ea.	60.00–65.00

Row 4: (Continued)

	#5	Refrigerator dish, 10" x 5", (Floral lid)	65.00– 75.00
Row 5:	#1-4	Spice canister, 3", ea.	70.00– 75.00
	#5	Child's size cannister "sugar" (others include coffee, cereal, tea)	225.00–250.00
	#6	Refrigerator dish, 4" x 4"	15.00– 18.00
	#7	Same, 4" x 8"	20.00– 25.00
Row 6:	#1	Batter jug (bottom only - $50.00)	295.00–325.00
	#2	Salt box	195.00–225.00
	#3	Reamer pitcher, 2 cup, light	30.00– 35.00
	#4	Same, dark (price varies as top & bottom match correctly)	75.00– 85.00

Page 44 (Jeannette Glass Co.)

Row 1:	#1, 2	Canister, round, screw-on lid, 40 oz. coffee, light or dark	85.00– 95.00
	#3	Same, sugar	85.00– 95.00
	#4, 5	Same, 16 oz., tea	45.00– 55.00
	#6	Vase	15.00– 18.00
Row 2:	#1, 3	Salt or pepper	12.00– 15.00
	#2	Drippings (no lettering - $20.00)	45.00– 55.00
	#4, 5	Flour or sugar	22.00– 25.00
	#6, 7	Decorated salt or pepper	15.00– 18.00
	#8-10	Bicarbonate soda or mouth wash	90.00–110.00
Row 3:	#1	Round crock, 40 oz., knob	40.00– 45.00
	#2	Tumbler, 12 oz.	20.00– 22.00
	#3	Sugar shaker, dark	65.00– 75.00
	#4	Sugar shaker, light	60.00– 70.00

Row 3: (Continued)

	#5	Round refrigerator dish, 32 oz.	22.00–25.00
Row 4:	#1	Bowl, 5½", horizontal rib	20.00–22.00
	#2	Bowl, 8", vertical rib	17.50–20.00
	#3	Same, 7"	15.00–18.00
	#4	Same, 6"	12.00–15.00
		Same, 9" (not shown)	20.00–22.00
Row 5:	#1	Match holder (lettering $30.00–35.00)	10.00–12.00
	#2	Ashtray	6.00– 8.00
	#3	Reamer, small, light	28.00–30.00
	#4	Same, dark	30.00–32.00
Row 6:	#1	Bowl, 9¾", horizontal rib	35.00–40.00
	#2	Same, 7½"	25.00–30.00
	#3	Bowl, 9¾", vertical rib	22.00–25.00

Page 45 (McKee Glass Co.)

Row 1:	#1-4	Canister, 48 oz., screw-on lid, ea.	55.00– 65.00
	#5	Bottoms down mug	145.00–155.00
	#6	Pitcher, 4 cup	30.00– 35.00
Row 2:	#1	Reamer, large	30.00– 35.00
	#2	Reamer, small	30.00– 35.00
	#3	Refrigerator dish, 4" x 5"	15.00– 18.00
	#4	Pitcher, 2 cup	15.00– 20.00
Row 3:	#1	Bowl, 9"	18.00– 20.00
		Same, 8" (not shown)	15.00– 18.00
		Same, 7" (not shown)	12.00– 15.00
		Same, 6" (not shown)	12.00– 15.00
	#2	Marked 'McK' pat. pend. (any ideas?)	10.00– 12.00
	#3	"Roman" arch side panel, salt	22.50– 25.00
	#5, 7	Same, cinnamon or spice	38.00– 42.00
	#4	Same, pepper	20.00– 25.00
	#6, 8	Flour and sugar	35.00– 38.00

Row 3: (Continued)

	#9	Tumbler or egg cup	12.00– 15.00
Row 4:	#1	"Tom & Jerry" bowl	75.00– 85.00
	#2	Measure cup, 2 spout	175.00– 195.00
	#3	Baker, 5" x 3½", oval	12.00– 15.00
	#4	Grapefruit reamer	150.00– 175.00
Row 5:	#1	"Tom & Jerry" mug	22.00– 25.00
	#2	Same, cup	25.00– 28.00
	#3	Egg beater bowl, w/spout	22.00– 25.00
	#4	Canister, round, 10 oz.	15.00– 18.00
		Same, 24 oz. (not shown)	20.00– 22.00
		Same, 40 oz. (not shown)	25.00– 28.00
	#5	Baker, 5" x 7", oval	15.00– 18.00
	#6	Custard cup	6.00– 10.00
Row 6:	#1	Measure pitcher, 4 cup, (sans handle)	400.00– 450.00
	#2-5	Canister, 28 oz., square, ea.	55.00– 65.00
	#6	Saunders reamer	1,250.00–1,450.00

44

GREEN TRANSPARENT ASSORTED ITEMS

The box of scoops shown below has been found in both crystal and green. I had purchased one green scoop of each size a few years ago; recently, a set in the original wooden enclosure was found. The individual scoops were already photographed for page 47, but I thought you might wish to see the whole set. The crystal set was found in an old hardware store with screws, nuts, and bolts residing therein. I suspect these were more practical for seeds, but going by the hunks of glass missing — maybe not. Notice the tissue holder on the second row of page 47, another unusual find.

Page 46

Row 1: #1 Small scoop   35.00–   40.00
       #2 Large scoop   50.00–   55.00
       #3 Set as pictured in box   750.00–1,000.00

Page 47

Row 1: #1 Cambridge oil and vinegar 85.00– 95.00
       #2 Paden City parfait   15.00– 18.00
       #3 Ice bucket w/metal drainer 45.00– 50.00
       #4 Georgian ice bucket   40.00– 45.00
Row 2: #1 Tissue holder   250.00–300.00
       #2 Moisture proof salt shaker 35.00– 40.00
       #3 Small scoop   35.00– 40.00
       #4 Large scoop   50.00– 55.00
Row 3: #1 Owens-Illinois shaker   7.50–   8.00
       #2 Tie back w/screw   10.00– 12.50
       #3-5 Assorted knobs, ea.   10.00– 12.50
       #6,7 Spoon and fork, set   40.00– 45.00
       #8 "Holt Soap Saver"; Duro
            Hock Co.; Chicago   15.00– 20.00

Row 3: (Continued)
       #9   Shaker   8.00– 10.00
Row 4: #1 Mixing bowl, 6½"   12.00– 15.00
       #2   Same, 5¾"   12.00– 15.00
       #3   "Tea Room" banana split   80.00– 90.00
       #4   Refrigerator dish ("To seal,
             turn cover to drop to slots") 22.50– 25.00
Row 5: #1 Mixing bowl, 9½"   25.00– 30.00
       #2,3 Heisey frosted spoon and
             fork   85.00–100.00
       #4   Pyrex casserole   20.00– 25.00
       #5,6 Cambridge spoon and
             fork set   100.00–110.00
       #7   U.S. Glass slick handle
             bowl w/cover   35.00– 40.00

47

GREEN TRANSPARENT, Jeannette, Hazel Atlas, Federal, and Others

Notice Fenton's "Ming" patterned reamer on page 50, Row 3, #4 that is not shown in the reamer section of the book. That coffee wall dispenser shown in the bottom row of page 51 is giving headaches to several trying to get one. Both items are luring collectors.

Page 49 All Jeannette Glass Co.

Row 1:	#1	"Hex Optic" reamer bucket	40.00– 45.00
	#2	Beater bowl	25.00– 30.00
	#3	Cruet, w/correct stopper	85.00– 90.00
	#4	Jenkins batter jug	135.00–150.00
Row 2:	#1	"Hex Optic" sugar shaker	175.00–195.00
	#2	Sugar shaker	100.00–110.00
	#3	Sugar shaker	70.00– 80.00
	#4	Mug	30.00– 35.00
	#5	Measure cup, tab handle	30.00– 35.00
	#6	2-cup measure (Sunflower bottom)	85.00– 95.00
Row 3:	#1	"Hex Optic" 4½" x 5" 'frige' jar	22.00– 25.00

Row 3:	(Continued)		
	#2	Same, dark	22.00– 25.00
	#3	Same, butter	75.00– 85.00
	#4	"Floral," 5" x 5"	65.00– 75.00
Row 4:	#1	Reamer, large	22.00– 25.00
	#2	Tab reamer	20.00– 25.00
	#3	Reamer top (fits pitcher or bucket)	20.00– 22.00
	#4	Butter	50.00– 55.00
Row 5:	#1	Covered 9" bowl	40.00– 45.00
	#2	Salt box, 6", "SALT" on lid	200.00–225.00
	#3	Butter, 2-lb. box	175.00–200.00

Page 50

Row 1:	#1	Paden City "Party Line" crushed fruit/cookie jar	65.00– 70.00
	#2-4	Cambridge set etched #732	200.00–250.00
Row 2:	#1	Stack sugar/creamer/plate	75.00– 85.00
	#2, 3	Marmalade, ea.	25.00– 28.00
	#4	Stack set: Westmoreland sugar creamer/plate/shakers	85.00– 95.00
	#5, 6	Curtain tie back, ea.	8.00– 10.00
	#7	Ash tray	8.00– 10.00
Row 3:	#1	Cambridge gravy & underliner	75.00– 85.00
	#2	Bowl, 7¾"	12.50– 15.00
	#3	Toothbrush holder, frosted	15.00– 18.00

Row 3:	(Continued)		
	#4	Fenton "Ming" reamer	500.00–600.00
	#5	Measure cup, 20 oz.	125.00–150.00
Row 4:	#1	Bottom to jar or canister	18.00– 20.00
	#2	Kompakt dish units, 8" x 4" (Pat. June 16, 1925)	65.00– 75.00
	#3	Towel bar	35.00– 40.00
	#4, 5	Curtain tie backs, pr.	18.00– 20.00
	#6-8	Drawer pulls, ea. (large backs $6.00–8.00); small backs	7.00– 8.00
	#9	Double drawer pull	18.00– 20.00

Page 51

Row 1:	#1	"Busy Betty" washing machine	250.00–300.00
	#2	Barrel cookie jar	60.00– 70.00
	#3	4-cup measure pitcher	700.00–750.00
	#4	Single doorknob	40.00– 45.00
	#5	Canister embossed COFFEE	120.00–130.00
Row 2:	#1	Rolling pin	450.00–500.00
	#2	"Zipper" canister embossed TEA	85.00–100.00

Row 3:	#1	Child's washboard embossed CRYSTAL	150.00–200.00
	#2	Double towel bar	35.00– 40.00
	#3	Double doorknob	100.00–110.00
Row 4:	#1, 5	Store shelf supports, ea.	25.00– 35.00
	#2	Pickle jar	110.00–125.00
	#3	Door hook (screw-in type)	22.00– 25.00
	#4	Wall coffee dispenser	400.00–450.00

GREEN TRANSPARENT, U.S. Glass, Tufglass, and Others

If anyone did know the purpose of the piece marked "ORASORB" (Row 1, #6), they didn't write. Everyone would like to know. Be wary of the embossed "salt or pepper" shown in Row 2. They have been reproduced in several colors including cobalt blue that was never made originally. The embossed "flour or sugar" have not been reproduced.

Page 53

Row 1:	#1	Canister, Hazel Atlas	40.00– 45.00
	#2	Canister, McKee (RARE)	55.00– 65.00
	#3, 4	Syrup, Hazel Atlas, ea.	30.00– 35.00
	#5	Syrup, Paden City	35.00– 40.00
	#6	"Orasorb" container	75.00– 80.00
Row 2:	#1, 2	Shaker, embossed salt or pepper	*30.00– 35.00
	#3, 4	Same, embossed flour or sugar	75.00– 85.00
	#5	FAN FOLD napkin holder	120.00–135.00
	#6	Measure cup, 3 spout, Federal	40.00– 45.00
	#7	Hazel Atlas tumbler	12.00– 15.00
	#8	Measure cup, Paden City	125.00–145.00
Row 3:	#1	Mixing bowl, 9"	22.00– 25.00

Row 3:		(Continued)	
		Same, 8" (not shown)	20.00–22.00
	#2	Same, 7"	18.00–20.00
	#3	Same, 6"	15.00–18.00
	#4	Same, 5"	15.00–18.00
Row 4:	#1	Butter, Hazel Atlas	50.00–55.00
	#2	Cheese plate ?	20.00–25.00
	#3	Measure cup (slightly oval)	55.00–65.00
	#4	Reamer top (scalloped edges)	45.00–50.00
Row 5:	#1	Fry tray 'Not heat resisting glass'	80.00–90.00
	#2	Lattice design refrigerator jar	22.00–25.00
	#3	Warming dish, two inserts	65.00–75.00

Page 54

Row 1:	#1	Sanitary jar	135.00–150.00
	#2	U.S. Glass reamer pitcher (snowflake in bottom)	65.00– 75.00
	#3	Slick-handled 9" covered bowl	35.00– 40.00
		w/o lid	15.00– 20.00
Row 2:	#1	Fluted sundae	22.00– 25.00
	#2	Soda	15.00– 18.00
	#3	Canning funnel	40.00– 45.00
	#4	Cruet	30.00– 35.00
	#5	Batter syrup (see page 81 Row 3 #2)	50.00– 55.00
	#6	U.S. Glass, 5" x 5"	18.00– 20.00

Row 3:	#1	Flask (hard day in kitchen!)	35.00– 45.00
	#2	"Tea Room" banana split	80.00– 90.00
	#3	Fluted sundae	22.50– 25.00
	#4	Cup, slick handle	10.00– 12.00
	#5	Banana split	20.00– 25.00
Row 4:	#1,3	Flat banana split, ea.	22.00– 27.00
	#2	9-oz. tumbler	10.00– 12.00
	#4	U.S. Glass covered dish	22.00– 25.00
Row 5:	#1,2	Salad set	85.00– 95.00
	#3	Spoon holder	175.00–200.00
	#4	Mug	20.00– 25.00

Tufglas
Page 55

Row 1:	#1	J.E. Marsden Glassworks mixing bowl, 5 pt., 10"	45.00– 50.00
	#2	Same, 3 pt., 9", made in Ambler, Pa.	40.00– 45.00
	#3	Same, 2 pt., 8", also not for oven use	35.00– 40.00
	#4	Same, 1½ pt., 7", for mixing, cooling & storing food	30.00– 35.00
Row 2:	#1	Butter dish	65.00– 70.00
	#2	Refrigerator dish, 3" x 6"	20.00– 25.00
	#3	Refrigerator dish, 6½" sq.	30.00– 35.00
	#4	"Tufglas Refrigerator Hydrator" No. 1	65.00– 70.00
Row 3:	#1	Tufglas tab-handled spouted bowl	35.00– 40.00
	#2	One-handled "No Splash Mixer"	40.00– 45.00
	#3	Measure pitcher, 36 oz.	140.00–160.00
	#4	Funnel	85.00– 95.00

Row 3:		(Continued)	
	#5	Custard, "Trade Mark Tufglas Registered"	8.00–10.00
Row 4:	#1	Reamer	85.00–95.00
	#2	Bowl, round, 4"	8.00–10.00
	#3	"Kold or Hot" small covered casserole	12.00–15.00
	#4	Jello mold	20.00–22.00
	#5	"Kold or Hot" Sanitary Food Mold	18.00–20.00
Row 5:	#1	4-cup "Kold or Hot" measure pitcher	55.00–65.00
	#2	Round refrigerator dish, "To seal, turn cover"	30.00–35.00
	#3	"Sanitary Butter Box," top only	30.00–35.00
	#4	Round bowl, wrinkled ridge, "Kold or Hot"	12.00–15.00
	#5	Custard w/ridges, "Kold or Hot"	2.00– 3.00

*See pages 236 – 237

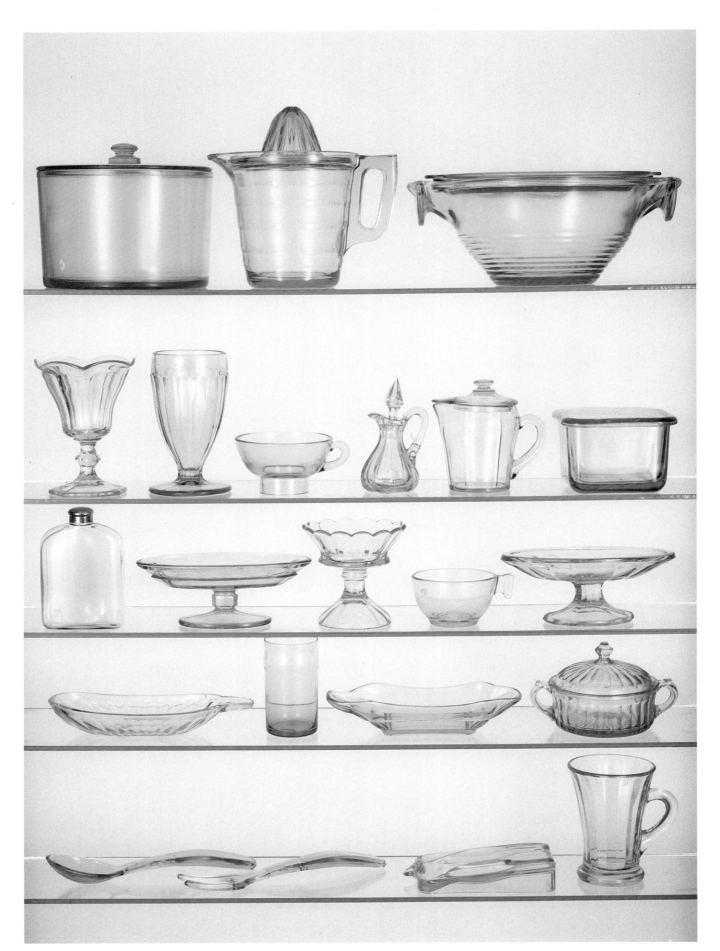

GREEN TRANSPARENT MISCELLANEOUS

Possibly the most coveted green canister set collectors are searching for is the Sneath set shown in Row 2, page 57. Very few sets have been completed over the years. The "Zipper" set shown in Row 3 is also very desirable, and can be found with less difficulty.

On page 58 in the bottom row is a Jenkins reamer pitcher set. It takes all three pieces to fetch the listed price.

Page 57

Row 1:	#1	Strawholder, tall	400.00–450.00
	#2	Strawholder, fancy base	450.00–500.00
	#3	Strawholder, short	375.00–400.00
	#4	Paden City, 'Rena' line tumbler	10.00– 12.00
	#5	Same, pitcher	35.00– 40.00
Row 2:	#1	Paden City syrup w/liner	60.00– 65.00
	#2	Bullet-shaped sugar shaker w/dots on top made by McKee	175.00–200.00
	#3-9	Sneath spice shakers, ea	40.00– 50.00
	#10	Sneath embossed TEA	175.00–200.00
	#11	Same, embossed COFFEE	250.00–275.00

Row 3:	#1	"Zipper" large canister	200.00–225.00
	#2	Same, embossed COFFEE	175.00–200.00
	#3	Same, embossed TEA	175.00–200.00
	#4-6	Same, spice shakers	35.00– 40.00
	#7	Holt soapsaver dish	20.00– 25.00
Row 4:	#1	Batter jug Paden City w/lid	65.00– 75.00
	#2	Paden City "Party Line" napkin holder	125.00–135.00
	#3	Pitcher	35.00– 45.00
	#4	Jenkins pitcher	50.00– 55.00

Page 58

Row 1:	#1	Canister, sugar	125.00–145.00
	#2	Cocktail shaker	22.00– 25.00
	#3	Ring cocktail shaker	22.50– 25.00
	#4	Apothecary jar	30.00– 35.00
	#5	Cookie, frosted	40.00– 45.00
Row 2:	#1	Spouted mixing bowl	20.00– 22.50
	#2	Butter tub	25.00– 30.00
	#3-5	Three jar set	60.00– 70.00
		w/black tray (not shown)	100.00–115.00
	#6	Mustard	15.00– 17.50
	#7	Spouted bowl, 4¹⁄₂"	20.00– 25.00

Row 3:	#1	Canister, similar to first item in Row 1	30.00– 35.00
	#2	Punch ladle	50.00– 55.00
	#3	Cambridge fork	50.00– 55.00
	#4	Knife rest	20.00– 22.00
Row 4:	#1	Jenkins reamer pitcher w/lid shown beside it	500.00–550.00
	#3	Canister embossed TEA	85.00– 95.00
	#4	Salt	85.00–100.00
	#5	Large salt	125.00–135.00

Page 59

Row 1:	#1	Churn	300.00–350.00
	#2	L.E. Smith cookie	110.00–125.00
	#3	Imperial cocktail shaker	60.00– 75.00
	#4	Cocktail shaker (Sweet Ad-Aline painted on side)	40.00– 45.00
Row 2:	#1	Reamer, called "Speakeasy" by collectors	35.00– 40.00
	#2	Hocking pinched-in decanter	65.00– 75.00
	#3	Cookie jar	40.00– 50.00
	#4	Jar	30.00– 35.00
	#5	Paden City ftd. tumbler	10.00– 12.00

Row 2:	(Continued)		
	#6	Glass straw	10.00–12.00
Row 3:	#1	Paden City sundae	20.00–22.00
	#2	Covered round dish, 7¹⁄₄"	27.50–30.00
	#3	Same, 8¹⁄₄"	32.50–35.00
	#4	Crock, 6¹⁄₄"	37.50–40.00
Row 4:	#1	Tufglas refrigerator dish, 5⁷⁄₈" sq.	20.00–25.00
	#2	Cold cream jar	8.00–10.00
	#3	Twisted towel bar	20.00–25.00
	#4	Coffee pot lid	10.00–12.00
	#5	Drawer pull	10.00–12.00

GREEN TRANSPARENT, Hocking Glass Company

The once plentiful supply of Hocking green is a thing of the past. New collectors are finding that many pieces are not to be found. The "Vegetable Freshener" (embossed on top) that is shown in Row 3 on page 63 is missing from many collections.

That water bottle in Row 1, #3, page 61 is more abundant than previously thought. Price has remained steady.

Page 61

Row 1:	#1	Decanter, pinched in	40.00– 45.00
	#2	Water bottle	25.00– 30.00
	#3	Water bottle	30.00– 35.00
	#4	Water bottle	22.00– 25.00
	#5	Decanter (same stopper as Cameo)	35.00– 40.00
Row 2:	#1-6	Pretzel Set (pitcher, jar, 4 mugs)	280.00–315.00
		Pitcher, 60 oz.	25.00– 30.00
		Pitcher, 80 oz. (not shown)	30.00– 35.00
		Mug, ea.	32.50– 35.00
		Pretzel jar	100.00–110.00
Row 3:	#1, 2	Water bottles, 32 oz., 2 styles	25.00– 30.00
	#3	Same, 62 oz.	25.00– 30.00
	#4, 5	Water bottles, raised panels, 32 oz	25.00– 30.00
		Same, 62 oz.	25.00– 30.00

Page 62

Row 1:	#1-3	Paneled mixing bowl, 11$^{1}/_{2}$"	30.00–35.00
		10$^{1}/_{4}$"	25.00–28.00
		9$^{1}/_{2}$"	22.00–25.00
Row 2:	#1, 3, 4	8$^{1}/_{2}$"	18.00–22.00
		7$^{1}/_{2}$"	12.00–15.00
		6$^{3}/_{4}$"	18.00–20.00
	#2	8$^{1}/_{2}$" bowl, embossed Diamond Crystal Salt	20.00–25.00
Row 3:	#1-4	Mixing bowl, 9$^{1}/_{2}$"	22.00–25.00
		8$^{3}/_{4}$"	18.00–22.00
		7$^{3}/_{4}$"	12.50–15.00
		6$^{3}/_{4}$"	12.00–15.00
Row 4:	#1	Mixing bowl, 10$^{1}/_{2}$"	22.00–25.00
	#2	Batter bowl, handled	30.00–35.00
	#3	Batter bowl	25.00–28.00

Page 63

Row 1:	#1	Butter dish	35.00– 40.00
	#2	Block Optic butter dish	50.00– 55.00
	#3	Refrigerator dish, Block design, 4$^{1}/_{4}$" x 4$^{3}/_{4}$"	25.00– 28.00
Row 2:	#1-3	Panelled refrigerator dish, 8" x 8"	30.00– 35.00
		Same, 4" x 8"	20.00– 25.00
		Same, 4" x 4"	17.50– 20.00
Row 3:	#1	"Vegetable Freshener" embossed on top	140.00–150.00
	#2, 3	Indent handle, 4" x 4", refrigerator dish	22.00– 25.00
		Same, 4" x 8"	30.00– 35.00
Row 4:	#1-4	Oval refrigerator jars (2 style knobs), 8"	30.00– 35.00
		Same, 7"	27.50– 30.00
		Same, 6"	22.50– 25.00
Row 5:	#1	Crock, 8"	40.00– 45.00
		Crock, 6$^{1}/_{2}$" (not shown)	30.00– 32.50
	#2	Crock, 5"	25.00– 27.50
	#3, 4	Round refrigerator jar and cover, 9"	25.00– 30.00
		Same, 7" (not shown)	22.00– 25.00
		Same, 5"	18.00– 20.00

GREEN TRANSPARENT and FIRED-ON COLORS,
Hocking and Others

Hocking canisters are the most popular of all those shown in this book, ostensibly because they can be found and the price is well within the range of most collectors. Finding canisters with perfect glass lids is a difficult task; the screw-type metal lid style is harder to find, but less in demand. In Florida, I prefer the screw-type because they are somewhat more moisture proof.

There is a 4-oz. provision jar to go with the other four in Row 3, page 65. I suspect that it is rare because it was never shown in Hocking's catalogues.

To save my answering letters, note that newly made labels for Hocking or Owens-Illinois canisters can be ordered from: Lorrie Kitchen, 3905F Torrance, Toledo, OH 43612. Write for price and styles if your labels are missing.

There are beginning to be more collectors for the fired-on colors. You will find additional photos of fired-on colors on pages 77 and 79.

Page 65

Row 1:	#1-5	Canisters, 47 oz. w/glass lid	50.00–55.00
	#6-8	Shakers, ea.	15.00–18.00
Row 2:	#1	Canister, screw-on lid, 64 oz.	50.00–55.00
	#2, 3	Same, 40 oz.	50.00–55.00
	#4	Same, 20 oz.	50.00–55.00
	#5	Shaker, 8 oz., labeled "Domino Sugar"	15.00–18.00
	#6, 7	Shakers, ea.	15.00–18.00
Row 3:	#1-4	Provision jars, 64 oz.	30.00–35.00
		Same, 32 oz.	22.50–25.00
		Same, 16 oz.	14.00–16.00

Row 3:	(Continued)		
		Same, 8 oz.	12.00–15.00
		Same, 4 oz. (not shown)	40.00–50.00
	#5, 7	Round shakers, pr.	50.00–60.00
	#6	Drip jar	40.00–45.00
Row 4:	#1	Canister	30.00–35.00
	#2-5	Smooth sided canister, 40 oz., screw-on lid	25.00–30.00
		Same, 20 oz.	25.00–30.00
		Same, 8 oz., ea.	12.00–15.00
	#6, 7	Shakers (sold individually as sugar shakers), ea.	25.00–30.00
	#8, 9	Milk bottle caps, ea.	4.00– 5.00

Page 66

Row 1:	#1	Cocktail shaker	22.50–25.00
	#2	Cocktail shaker (pinched-in sides)	25.00–30.00
	#3	Onion chopper	22.00–25.00
	#4	Cigarette jar, ash tray on top	18.00–20.00
	#5	Toothpick	18.00–20.00
	#6	Electric beater	25.00–30.00
Row 2:	#1	Measure cup	75.00–85.00
	#2-4	Measure cups, ea.	30.00–35.00
	#5	Syrup	30.00–35.00
	#6	Cruet	20.00–25.00
	#7	Ash tray	8.00–10.00

Row 3:	#1	2-piece reamer	30.00–35.00
	#2	Reamer pitcher	25.00–30.00
	#3	2-piece reamer-ribbed pitcher	60.00–65.00
	#4	2-piece reamer	35.00–40.00
Row 4:	#1	Reamer, odd shade	25.00–30.00
	#2	"Coke" bottle green	20.00–25.00
	#3	Reamer, shade most collected	25.00–30.00
	#4	Tab-handled reamer	22.00–25.00
	#5	Tab-handled reamer	22.00–25.00

Page 67

Row 1:	#1	Canister, glass lid, black	25.00–30.00
	#2	Canister, Tulip design	15.00–20.00
	#3	Canister (rabbits, ducks, lambs)	15.00–20.00
	#4	Checkerboard sugar	20.00–25.00
	#5	Same, flour	22.50–25.00
Row 2:	#1-4	Shakers, black, ea.	10.00–12.00
	#5-7	Shakers, red, ea.	10.00–12.00
	#8	Shaker, green	8.00–10.00
	#9	Crisscross, 5¼" bowl	12.00–15.00
Row 3:	#1	Canister, screw-on lid, green	15.00–20.00

Row 3:	(Continued)		
	#2	Fire-King, 4⅞" bowl, green	3.50– 5.00
	#3	Same, 6", red	4.50– 5.00
		Same 7¼" (not shown)	7.00– 9.00
	#4	Same, 8⅜", blue	10.00–12.00
Row 4:	#1-4	Shakers, ea	4.00– 5.00
	#5	Bowl, 10¼"	18.00–20.00
	#6	Syrup, green rings	15.00–18.00
	#7	Marmalade, red ring w/spoon	15.00–18.00

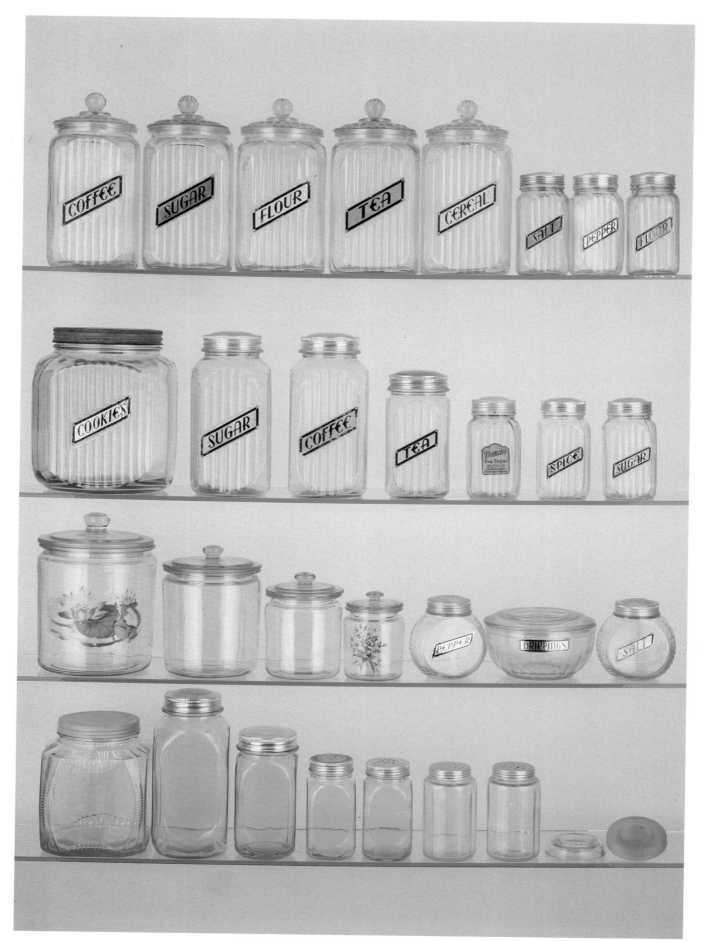

PINK

That pair of embossed salt and pepper shakers on page 72 Row 5 have been reproduced in pink, green, and cobalt blue; the latter was never made originally. See Reproduction Section on pages 236-237 for items with asterisk.

Some of the pink items you need to watch for include: "Tricia" reamer (page 69 Row 4, # 4); Paramount napkin holder (page 71 Row 2, #2); "Ming" reamer (page 71 Row 3, #3) and the dispenser mentioned in the next paragraph. I imagine that you could look at the prices and surmise that on your own.

It turns out that the "so-called" sugar dispenser shown on page 69 Row 4, #5 and (shown complete on page 71 Row 2, #1) is a liquid dispenser for syrup or soap.

Row 1:	#1	Hex Optic stack set, Jeannette; base ($12.50–15.00);	
		lid ($18.00–20.00)	55.00– 65.00
	#2	Hex Optic flat-rim mixing bowl, 9"	25.00– 30.00
		Same, 10" (not shown)	27.50– 30.00
		Same, 8¼" (not shown)	20.00– 25.00
		Same, 7¼" (not shown)	16.00– 20.00
	#3	Hex Optic ruffled-edge mixing bowl, 8¼"	22.50– 25.00
		Same, 10½" (not shown)	27.50– 30.00
		Same, 6" (not shown)	20.00– 22.00
	#4	Ice bucket w/lid, Fry	175.00–200.00
Row 2:	#1	Butter box, 2 lb. embossed "B," Jeannette	160.00–180.00
	#2	Round salt	200.00–225.00
	#3, 4	Flat Jennyware shakers, pr.	60.00– 70.00
	#5	Tumbler	12.00– 15.00
	#6	Cruet	35.00– 40.00
	#7	Barber bottle	22.00– 25.00
Row 3:	#1, 2	Moisture proof shakers, pr.	165.00–185.00
	#3	Reamer, probably foreign	40.00– 45.00
		Same, sun-colored amethyst (not shown)	35.00– 45.00
		Same, crystal (not shown)	20.00– 25.00
	#4	Tumbler, imprinted Mission Juice	25.00– 30.00
	#5, 6	Quilted refrigerator jars, w/lid 8 oz.	25.00– 27.50
		4 oz.	17.50– 20.00
	#7	Stack sugar, creamer and lid	50.00– 60.00
	#8	Same only with place for salt and pepper	35.00– 40.00
		Set w/salt and pepper on above	75.00– 85.00
Row 4:	#1	MacBeth Evans stack set	50.00– 60.00
	#2	Ice bucket	30.00– 35.00
	#3	Ice bucket w/Sterling bear	35.00– 40.00
	#4	Reamer called "Tricia" by collectors	700.00–800.00
	#5	Dispenser w/insert (insert not shown)	150.00–175.00
Row 5:	#1	Reamer, unembossed "Orange Juice Extractor"	185.00–200.00
	#2	Paden City syrup jug	45.00– 50.00
	#3	New Martinsville syrup jug	50.00– 60.00
	#4, 5	Heisey Twist cruet, 2½ oz.	70.00– 75.00
		4 oz.	75.00– 80.00
	#6	Heisey Twist mustard w/spoon	75.00– 80.00
		w/o spoon	40.00– 50.00
	#7	Cambridge syrup	55.00– 65.00
Row 6:	#1	Bowl, 9¾" marked Cambridge	25.00– 30.00
	#2	Bowl, 7¾" plain bottom	20.00– 22.00
	#3	Bowl, 8", concentric rings in bottom	20.00– 22.00
	#4	Butter dish, bow-handled top	50.00– 60.00

PINK (Continued)

Page 71

Row 1: #1   Paden City "Party Line"
             crushed fruit/cookie jar   60.00– 70.00
     #2   Jenkins batter pitcher   150.00–175.00
     #3   Cambridge batter jug for
             waffle set   80.00– 90.00
     #4   Cocktail shaker   70.00– 80.00
Row 2: #1   Dispenser (possibly liquid
             soap or syrup)   150.00–175.00
     #2   Paramount napkin holder
             (U.S. Glass)   400.00–450.00
     #3   U.S. Glass "SHARI" cosmetic
             holder (2 pc.)   125.00–150.00
     #4   Stack set: sugar/creamer/
             plate/shakers   75.00– 85.00

Row 3: #1   Cambridge double gravy boat   40.00– 45.00
     #2   Imperial gravy boat   30.00– 35.00
     #3   Fenton "Ming" 2-piece reamer   500.00–600.00
     #4   Tufglas jello mold   40.00– 50.00
Row 4: #1   Paden City Party Line ice tub   25.00– 30.00
     #2   U.S. Glass 2-cup measure   175.00–200.00
     #3   Cambridge 1-cup measure   225.00–250.00
     #4   Stack sugar/creamer/lid   50.00– 60.00
     #5, 6   Curtain tie backs, ea.   8.00– 10.00
Row 5: #1, 2   Curtain tie backs, ea.   11.00– 14.00
     #3   Drawer pull, single   10.00– 15.00
     #4, 5   Single towel rods, 18", ea.   25.00– 30.00
     #6   Double towel rod   35.00– 40.00

Page 72

Hocking Glass Company

Row 1: #1   Pretzel jar   85.00–95.00
     #2-4   Canisters, plain, 40 oz.   40.00–50.00
             20 oz. (not shown)   35.00–40.00
             8 oz.   30.00–35.00
     #5   Refrigerator dish, 4" x 4",
             indented handles   22.00–25.00
     #6   Measure pitcher, 2 cup,
             ribbed   50.00–55.00

Federal Glass Company

Row 2: #1-4   Mixing bowl set (4)   55.00–68.00
             $9^1/2$"   18.00–20.00
             $8^1/2$"   15.00–18.00
             $7^1/2$"   12.00–15.00
             $6^1/2$"   12.00–15.00
Row 3: #1, 2 &
     4   Refrigerator dish set (3)   78.00–90.00
             8" x 8"   35.00–40.00
             4" x 8"   25.00–30.00
             4" x 4"   18.00–20.00
     #3   Refrigerator dish,
             $3^3/4$" x $5^3/4$", w/legs   20.00–25.00
     #5   Butter dish, ¼ lb.   32.50–38.00
Row 4: #1   Butter dish, 1 lb.   40.00–42.50
     #2   4" x 4" vegetable embossed
             lid (asparagus)   22.00–25.00

Row 4: (Continued)
             4" x 8" vegetable embossed
             lid (not shown)   30.00– 35.00
     #3, 4   Round refrigerator dish, $4^1/2$"   15.00– 20.00
             Same, $5^1/2$"   12.00– 15.00
     #5   Reamer, Federal   90.00–100.00

Hazel Atlas Glass Company

Row 5: #1, 2   Mixing bowls, $11^5/8$"
             (not shown)   25.00– 30.00
             $10^5/8$" (not shown)   22.00– 25.00
             $9^5/8$"   18.00– 20.00
             $8^5/8$" (not shown)   15.00– 18.00
             $7^5/8$"   12.00– 15.00
             $6^5/8$" (not shown)   12.00– 15.00
     #3, 4   Salt or pep, embossed   *40.00– 45.00
     #5   Cruet   50.00– 55.00
     #6   Milk pitcher   30.00– 35.00
Row 6: #1-4   REST-WELL mixing bowl
             set (5)   74.00– 90.00
             $9^1/2$"   20.00– 25.00
             $8^1/2$"   18.00– 20.00
             $7^1/2$"   12.00– 15.00
             $6^1/2$" (not shown)   12.00– 15.00
             $5^1/2$"   12.00– 15.00

Page 73

Row 1: #1   Utility pitcher   50.00–60.00
     #2   Slick-handle measure pitcher   40.00–45.00
     #3   Measure cup   50.00–60.00
     #4   Cruet   45.00–50.00
     #5   Cruet   40.00–50.00
     #6   Apothecary jar   22.00–25.00
Row 2: #1   Heisey cigarette and ash tray   65.00–75.00
     #2   Cruet set   80.00–90.00
     #3   Mixing bowl, 7"   16.00–20.00
             Same, 5"   12.50–15.00
             Same, 9"   20.00–25.00
     #4   Mug, "Adams Rib"   20.00–25.00
     #5   Ice pail   20.00–25.00
Row 3: #1   Round crock, 8", lid fits outside   35.00–40.00
     #2   Same, $6^1/2$"   25.00–30.00
     #3   Round refrigerator dish, tab
             handle   25.00–30.00

Row 3: (Continued)
     #4   "Kompakt" dish unit   50.00–60.00
Row 4: #1   Slick-handle mixing bowl,
             $8^3/4$" w/lid, spouted   40.00–45.00
             Same w/o lid   20.00–25.00
     #2   Slick-handle mixing bowl,
             9", (2 handles, spouted)   22.00–25.00
             Same w/lid   40.00–45.00
     #3   Slick handle bowl, $7^1/2$",
             spouted, "D&B" embossed   25.00–30.00
Row 5: #1   Slick handle 9" concentric
             ring bowl   22.00–25.00
             Same, w/lid   35.00–40.00
     #2   Snowflake cake plate   22.00–25.00
     #3   2-handle bowl, no spout, 9"   22.00–25.00

RED, TRANSPARENT and FIRED-ON COLORS

I've seen few red kitchens around, but red is a dramatic accent color; so there is a lot of demand for the red pieces shown here and on the next page. Fired-on colors really photograph nicely as you can see on page 77.

Page 75

Row 1: #1	Boot cocktail shaker	250.00–300.00
#2	Silex coffee pot	175.00–200.00
#3	Decanter w/shot glass stopper	100.00–110.00
Row 2: #1	Cocktail shaker	50.00– 55.00
#2	3 oz. tumbler that goes w/#1	8.00– 10.00
#3	Barbell cocktail shaker (possibly New Martinsville)	85.00– 95.00

Row 2: (Continued)		
#4	Duncan Miller cocktail shaker	50.00– 55.00
#5	Cocktail shaker	50.00– 55.00
Row 3: #1	McKee batter pitcher	100.00–125.00
#2	Batter pitcher w/tray	175.00–200.00
#3, 4	Tumble-up set	175.00–200.00

Page 76

Row 1: #1	Hocking tumbler w/Old Reliable tea bags	10.00– 12.00
#2, 3	Hocking water bottles, plain or ribbed	175.00–200.00
#4	Food chopper	20.00– 25.00
#5	Strawholder (possibly 60's)	150.00–200.00
#6	Hocking 24 oz. beater jar	40.00– 45.00
Row 2: #1	Cambridge "Mt. Vernon" ice bucket	75.00– 85.00
#2	Hocking ice bucket	30.00– 35.00
#3	Cruet	100.00–120.00
#4	Sugar shaker (maybe 60's)	175.00–200.00
#5, 6	Wheaton Nuline shakers, pr.	40.00– 50.00
#7, 8	Hocking shakers (possibly 60's), pr.	35.00– 45.00

Row 3: #1	Imperial gravy & platter	150.00–175.00
#2	Butter w/crystal top	105.00–120.00
#3	Mixing bowl set (3)	190.00–220.00
	9¼"	90.00–100.00
	7¾"	60.00– 70.00
	6½"	40.00– 50.00
Row 4: #1	Percolator top	15.00– 17.50
#2	Knob escutcheon plate for door knob	10.00– 12.00
#3	Double drawer pull	35.00– 45.00
#4	Single drawer pull	20.00– 25.00
#5, 6	Curtain rings, ea.	10.00– 12.00
#7, 8	Feathered curtain tie backs, pr.	25.00– 35.00
Row 5: #1	Trivet	40.00– 50.00
#2	Tray (possibly for a New Martinsville set)	45.00– 50.00
#3, 4	Fork & spoon set	175.00–200.00

Page 77

Row 1: #1, 2	Rooster decanter w/4 shots	35.00–40.00
#3	Sugar shaker (Gemco)	18.00–20.00
#4	Canister, blue	15.00–18.00
#5	Rooster canister, small	20.00–25.00
#6	Same, medium	25.00–30.00
#7	Same, large	35.00–40.00
Row 2: #1	Measure, 2 cup	10.00–12.00
#2	Pyrex, refrigerator jar, 3½" x 4¾"	4.00– 5.00
#3	Hazel Atlas cup, green	32.00–35.00
#4	Same, red	35.00–40.00
#5, 6	Hocking ribbed shakers, blue, ea.	8.00–10.00
Row 3: #1-3	Hocking, yellow, ea.	7.00– 9.00
#4-6	Same, blue, ea.	10.00–12.00
#7-10	Same, green, ea.	9.00–11.00

Row 4: #1-5	Roman arch side panel, ea.	8.00–10.00
#6	Glasbake, red cup	25.00–30.00
#7, 8	Shakers, ea	4.00– 5.00
#9	Reamer, tab handle, red	12.00–15.00
Row 5: #1	Oval 7" jar, black	15.00–18.00
#2, 3	Shaker (go with #1-3 in Row 4)	5.00– 6.00
#4	Rolling pin, white	25.00–30.00
Row 6: #1	Mustard (Gemco set)	4.00– 5.00
#2	Salt bowl, same	8.00–10.00
#3	Sugar shaker, same	15.00–20.00
#4	Hazel Atlas sugar canister	25.00–30.00
#5	Same, coffee	20.00–25.00
#6	Same, tea	18.00–20.00
#7	Hocking tea canister	12.50–15.00

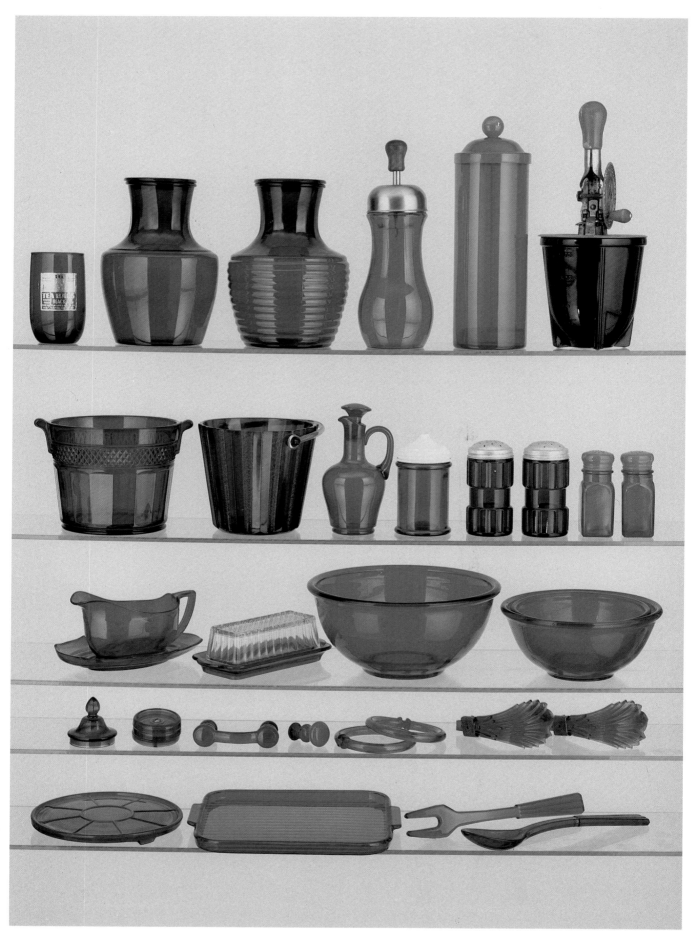

77

FIRED-ON COLORS (Continued)

Isn't this a super photo! I hope it shows the awesome display potential for collecting fired-on colors, which are abundantly available! Red and green items have traditionally been my best sellers over the years.

The blue windmill drippings jar in Row 2 was re-photographed since it had been turned so you could not see the word "Drippings" in the last book. Much to my chagrin, upon viewing the new photographs from a six day marathon photo shoot last October, the "Drippings" label had been turned to the back again! Someday we will get it right.

Page 79

Row 1:	#1-#4	Shakers, ea.	5.00– 6.00
	#5	Cup w/red handle	4.00– 5.00
	#6	Black shaker	8.00–10.00
	#7	Small sugar shaker	12.00–14.00
	#8	Small striped canister	5.00– 6.00
Row 2:	#1	Dutch bowl, 7"	8.00–10.00
	#2	Dutch cereal, 5"	6.00– 8.00
	#3	Oil or vinegar bottle	8.00–10.00
	#4	Apothecary jar	10.00–12.00
	#5	Drippings jar (turned backwards)	30.00–35.00
	#6	Glasbake measure pitcher	25.00–30.00
Row 3:	#1	Hazel Atlas flour canister (goes w/set page 77 Row 6)	25.00–30.00
	#2,6	Syrup, ea.	12.50–15.00
	#3	Batter bowl	12.50–15.00
	#4	Knobs, ea.	6.00– 8.00
	#4	Carafe	4.00– 5.00
Row 4:	#1-4	Pyrex bowl set	20.00–28.00
	#1	Yellow	8.00–10.00
	#2	Red	6.00– 8.00
	#3	Green	4.00– 6.00
	#4	Blue	2.00– 4.00
Row 5:	#1,2	Multi-colored soup cups, ea.	2.50– 4.00
	#3	Pyrex 3½" x 4¾" yellow refrigerator dish	3.00– 4.00
	#4	Pyrex 4¼" x 6¾" blue refrigerator dish	5.00– 7.00
	#5	Cobalt tumbler w/red, white Dutch scene	12.50–15.00
	#6	Crystal pitcher w/Dutch scene	20.00–25.00
	#7	Same as #4, red	6.00– 8.00
	#8	Same as #3, orange	3.00– 4.00
	#9	Pyrex 7" x 9", yellow refrigerator dish	8.00–10.00

WHITE

White kitchenware is very versatile in a decorating scheme and more abundant than many colors! Prices reflect that abundance; so, today's collectors are using this color in their kitchens.

The napkin holder in the bottom row on Page 81 is marked "HY-G NAPKINS." It is the only one I have seen!

Page 81

Row 1: #1,2 Salt and "white pepper" pr. 12.00–15.00
     #3 Musketeer "Allspice" 10.00–12.00
     #4,5 Salt and pepper "4 Rings," pr. 12.00–15.00
     #6 "Home Soap Company" shaker
     #7 "Red Tulips" Vitrock grease jar 20.00–25.00
     #8,10 "Red Tulips" salt or pepper, ea. 10.00–12.50
     #9 "Red Tulips" sugar 15.00–17.50

Row 2: #1 Chicken sherbet 10.00–12.50
     #2,3 Salt and pepper pr. 10.00–12.00
     #4 Anchor Hocking mug, chicken decal 5.00– 6.00
     #5 Hazel Atlas mug, chef scene 8.00–10.00
     #6,7 Drawer pulls, ea. 4.00– 5.00
     #8 McKee "FRIZZ" bowl (Just 1. Chill; 2. Whip; 3. Freeze) 30.00–35.00

Row 3: #1-18 Griffith's shakers (w/label) ea. 1.50– 2.50
     #1-18 Griffith's shakers (wo/label) ea. 1.00– 1.25

Row 4: #1 Hazel Atlas "Dutch, tulips, windmills" plate (goes with set shown on page 231) 6.00– 8.00
     #2 Same, cup and saucer 12.50–15.00
     #3 Rooster bowl 5.00– 6.00
     #4 McKee, Glasbake coffee pot 30.00–35.00
     #5 Hazel Atlas, 4 cup measure, stippled exterior 20.00– 25.00

Row 5: #1,2 Canisters, decaled cherry or vegetables, ea. 15.00– 17.50
     #3 Canisters, decaled vegetables 14.00– 16.00
     #4 Hazel Atlas "Dots" tumbler 12.50– 15.00
     #5 Syrup 30.00– 35.00
     #3 Napkin holder marked "HY-G NAPKINS" 125.00–150.00

* BEWARE REPRODUCTIONS

Page 82 McKee Glass Company

Row 1: #1-4 Canister, 48 oz., ea 50.00– 55.00
     #5-8 Large shakers, ea 45.00– 50.00

Row 2: #1-4 Shakers, ea. 15.00– 18.00
     #5,6 Salt, pepper, ea. 18.00– 20.00
     #7,8 Flour, sugar, ea. 22.00– 25.00
     #9 Canister, same design 60.00– 75.00
     #10 Dots 48 oz. canister 60.00– 75.00

Row 3: #1 Grapefruit reamer 250.00–350.00
     #2 Tea w/lid 25.00– 30.00
     #3 Bowl, 9" w/decal 20.00– 25.00
     #4 2 cup measure w/decal 30.00– 35.00

Row 4: #1 Bowl, 9" 18.00– 20.00
     #2, 3 Shakers (good lettering!) 15.00– 18.00
     #4 Reamer, small 20.00– 25.00
     #5 Sunkist reamer 7.00– 10.00

Row 5: #1 Water dispenser 110.00–125.00
     #2 Glasbak measure cup 60.00– 75.00
     #3 Shakers, salt 12.00– 15.00
     #4,5 Shaker, flour or sugar 20.00– 25.00
     #6 Diamond Check shaker 17.50– 20.00

Page 83 Hocking Glass Company Vitrock

Row 1: #1 Canister w/glass lid (rare) 75.00–85.00
     #2 Canister, 20 oz. screw-on lid 30.00–35.00
     #3 Shaker 12.00–15.00
     #4-5 Mixing bowl, $6^3/4$" 6.00– 8.00
     Same, $7^1/2$" (not shown) 8.00–10.00
     Same, $8^1/2$" (not shown) 10.00–12.50
     Same, $9^1/2$" (not shown) 12.50–15.00
     Same, $10^1/2$" (not shown) 18.00–20.00
     Same, $11^1/4$" 22.50–25.00

Row 2: #1 "Blue Circle" flour 27.50–30.00
     #2-5 Same, shakers, ea. 12.00–15.00
     #6, 7 "Black Circle" shakers, ea. 12.00–15.00

Row 3: #1 Grease w/o label 22.00–25.00
     Same, w/label 20.00–25.00
     #2 2 cup measure w/lid 30.00–40.00
     #3 Reamer 20.00–25.00
     #4 Bowl, 10", red trim 22.00–25.00

Row 4: #1-3 "Red Circle" w/screw-on lids 40.00–45.00
     #4-6 Same, shakers, ea. 12.00–15.00

Row 5: #1 "Red Circle w/flowers," canister w/screw-on lid 35.00–40.00
     #2 Tab handle reamer 85.00–100.00
     #3 4" x 4" refrigerator dish 15.00–18.00
     #4 8" x 8" refrigerator dish 32.50–35.00

YELLOW, OPAQUE, and TRANSPARENT, McKee, Hocking
and Others

McKee's opaque yellow is called "Seville." This color is sometimes confused with Custard by beginning collectors. Custard leans to the white with a beige tint while "Seville" **is** yellow. Page 85 gives a representative example of this color that can be compared to Hocking's opaque yellow shown on page 86. Even though Hocking's yellow is more rare, there are fewer collectors; and that limits its price potential. Most yellow opaque pieces are found with black lettering, but there are exceptions to that rule. Some Hocking pieces have been seen with green lettering! Price the cookie jar below for $250.00 – 300.00.

Page 85 McKee Glass Company

Row 1:	#1	Pinch decanter	100.00–110.00	Row 3:	#1 Grapefruit reamer	210.00–225.00
	#2	Measure, 4 cup, no handle	400.00–450.00		#2 Sunkist reamer	45.00– 55.00
	#3	Measure, 4 cup, ftd. w/handle	115.00–130.00		#3 Refrigerator dish, 7¼" square	30.00– 35.00
	#4	4 cup dry measure (mug)	150.00–200.00	Row 4:	#1 Butter dish	65.00– 75.00
Row 2:	#1	Bottoms down mug	135.00–150.00		#2 4" x 5" refrigerator dish	15.00– 18.00
	#2	Measure, 2 cup	30.00– 35.00		#3 Measure cup, 2 spout	175.00–195.00
	#3-9	Salt or pepper, ea.	15.00– 20.00		#4 Bowl, 4¼"	10.00– 12.00
		Flour or sugar, ea.	20.00– 25.00	Row 5:	#1 Mixing bowl, 9¼"	22.50– 25.00
					#2 Same, 7½"	18.00– 20.00
					#3,4 Canister, 48 oz., ea.	55.00– 60.00

Page 86 Hocking Glass Company

Row 1:	#1-3	Canister, 40 oz., ea.	65.00–75.00	Row 3:	#1 Measure pitcher	175.00–200.00
	#4,5	Canister, 20 oz., ea.	30.00–35.00		#2 Batter bowl	75.00– 85.00
Row 2:	#1	Refrigerator jar, 4" x 4"	12.00–15.00	Row 4:	#1 Refrigerator dish, 8" x 8"	40.00– 50.00
		Same, w/lid	18.00–20.00		#2, 4 Salt or pepper	16.00– 20.00
	#2,3	Shaker, flour or sugar	22.00–25.00		#3 Grease jar	40.00– 45.00
	#4	Refrigerator dish, 6" x 6"	20.00–22.50			

Yellow Transparent
Page 87

Row 1:	#1	Fenton ice bucket	125.00–135.00	Row 4:	(Continued)	
	#2	U.S. Glass reamer pitcher	650.00–750.00		#3 Same, 6¾"	22.00–25.00
	#3	Glass for above set	15.00– 17.50		#4 Same, 5¾"	18.00–20.00
	#4	Fostoria ice bucket	30.00– 35.00	Row 5:	#1 U.S. Glass slick handled batter bowl	30.00–35.00
	#5	Fostoria oil and vinegar	65.00– 75.00		#2 Soap dish	18.00–20.00
	#6	Fostoria "Mayfair" cruet	75.00– 85.00		#3 Cambridge sugar cube tray	65.00–75.00
Row 2:	#1	Fostoria oil and vinegar	45.00– 50.00		#4 Spoon, salad size	30.00–35.00
	#2	Fostoria "Mayfair" syrup & liner	65.00– 70.00		#5 Spoon, regular size	25.00–30.00
	#3	Sugar shaker	300.00–350.00			
	#4	Hazel Atlas 2 cup reamer set	300.00–325.00			
	#5	Hazel Atlas mug	30.00– 35.00			
	#6	Duncan "Festive" gravy & ladle	40.00– 50.00			
Row 3:	#1	Heisey syrup	85.00– 95.00			
	#2	Heisey "Old Sandwich"	85.00– 95.00			
	#3	Hazel Atlas 1 cup measure, 3 spout	250.00–295.00			
	#4	Hazel Atlas egg cup	5.00– 8.00			
	#5	Canning funnel "C.W. Hart," Troy, N.Y.	35.00– 45.00			
	#6	Hazel Atlas refrigerator dish 4½" x 5"	30.00– 35.00			
Row 4:	#1	Hazel Atlas REST-WELL, mixing bowl, 8¾"	35.00– 40.00			
	#2	Same, 7¾"	30.00– 35.00			

SALT PEPPER SUGAR FLOUR SALT FLOUR SUGAR

CEREAL TEA

85

Part 2 Kitchen Items

BATTER JUGS and BATTER BOWLS

Batter jugs were usually made in sets consisting of a batter jug and lid, syrup and lid and drip tray. Although these sets were made by several different companies in a myriad of colors, cobalt blue and red are the most popular colors with collectors.

Page 91 shows a collection of batter bowls. They came in many shapes and sizes, although all those shown were made by Hocking. The "Mayfair" blue in Row 2 and the "Turquoise Blue" in Row 4 are most coveted by collectors. It took us four years to find the "Turquoise Blue" when we were collecting that color.

The Hocking canister in Row 3 was a late arrival, and since this was an all Hocking page I included it there. The top shows that "ARCO" Coffee was in the jar; but when empty, the jar was to become your cookies' home.

Page 89

Row 1:	#1	Paden City crystal w/black lids set	125.00–150.00
	#2	Paden City black set	275.00–295.00
	#3	Paden City pink w/black tray set	175.00–195.00
Row 2:	#1	Paden City syrup	50.00– 60.00
	#2	Paden City batter jug	60.00– 70.00
	#3	Paden City milk jug	55.00– 65.00
	#4	Paden City green batter jug	65.00– 75.00
	#5	Cambridge pink batter jug for waffle set	75.00– 85.00
	#6	Cambridge amber syrup jug	50.00– 55.00

Row 3:	#1	Jenkins #570 green batter jug	135.00–150.00
	#2	Green batter jug	110.00–125.00
	#3	Square green batter jug	125.00–150.00
	#4	Jenkins green batter jug	200.00–225.00
Row 4:	#1	Jenkins pink batter jug	135.00–150.00
	#2	Jeannette Jadite (bottom only- $50.00)	250.00–285.00
	#3	Liberty "American Pioneer" batter jug	150.00–165.00
	#4	Same, syrup jug	125.00–140.00

Page 90

Row 1:	#1	New Martinsville cobalt blue batter set	300.00–350.00
	#2	Same, amber	150.00–175.00
	#3	Red batter jug & liner	175.00–200.00
Row 2:	#1	New Martinsville green batter jug	65.00– 75.00
	#2	Same, syrup jug	60.00– 65.00
	#3	New Martinsville crystal batter w/green top	30.00– 40.00

Row 2:	(Continued)		
	#4	New Martinsville pink syrup jug	40.00– 50.00
Row 3:	#1	McKee black batter	110.00–125.00
	#2	Same, white	75.00– 85.00
	#3	Same, blue	100.00–125.00
	#4	Same, red	110.00–125.00

Page 91 All Anchor Hocking Glass Company

Row 1:	#1	Ribbed green	30.00– 35.00
	#2	Opaque yellow	75.00– 85.00
Row 2:	#1	Ribbed crystal	15.00– 18.00
	#2	Spiraled green	30.00– 35.00
	#3	"Mayfair" blue	250.00–300.00

Row 3:	#1	Cookie jar w/coffee lid	50.00– 55.00
	#2	Fire-King (peach/grape)	20.00– 25.00
Row 4:	#1	Same, Jadite	20.00– 22.00
	#2	Same, "Turquoise Blue"	200.00–250.00

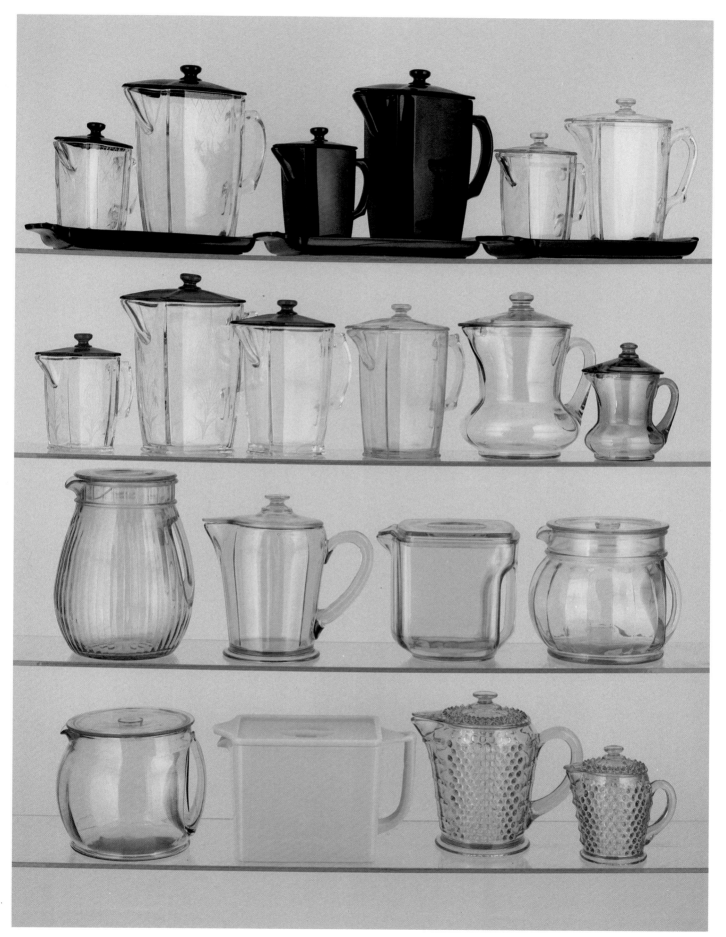

BUTTER DISHES, CHEESE DISHES, and CANISTERS

Butter dishes can be found in several sizes and shapes from quarter pound to two pounds. Many were premium items as indicated by the advertising found imprinted or embossed on them. In Row 2, #4 on page 93, the top says "Ask for Iowa creamery butter, always good!" So many older canisters are finding their way into today's kitchens that I have included a page of some odd ones. After all, it was canisters with screw-on lids that Cathy began buying 15 years ago that eventually evolved into this book.

Page 93

Row 1:	#1	Custard, McKee	40.00– 45.00
	#2	Skokie green, McKee	45.00– 50.00
	#3	Seville yellow, McKee	60.00– 65.00
Row 2:	#1	Ships, McKee	30.00– 35.00
	#2	Red Dots	100.00–125.00
	#3	Delphite, McKee	300.00–325.00
	#4	Jadite bottom, metal top ad	25.00– 30.00
Row 3:	#1,2	Amber 1/4 lb., Federal, ea.	30.00– 35.00
	#3	Crystal frosted, 1/4 lb. Federal	22.00– 25.00
	#4	Amber 1 lb., Federal	30.00– 35.00
	#5	Amber tub, Federal	25.00– 30.00
Row 4:	**Jeannette** tops embossed "BUTTER"		
	#1	Delphite,	250.00–300.00

Row 4:	(Continued)		
	#2	Jadite, dark,	50.00– 55.00
	#3	Jadite, light,	50.00– 55.00
	#4	Green,	50.00– 55.00
	#5	Pink, (all pink)	60.00– 70.00
Row 5:	#1	Ultra-marine, "Jennyware"	150.00–175.00
	#2	Same, crystal	125.00–150.00
	#3	Same, pink	150.00–175.00
	#4	Pink, embossed Scotty	35.00– 40.00
Row 6:	#1	Green, embossed "B," 2 lb.	150.00–175.00
	#2	Green, "Hex Optic"	65.00– 85.00
	#3	Pink, embossed "B," 2 lb.	160.00–185.00

Page 94

Row 1:	#1	Green, unknown	45.00– 50.00
	#2	Green, Hocking	40.00– 45.00
	#3	Green, "Block Optic," Hocking	50.00– 55.00
Row 2:	#1	Green, unknown	50.00– 55.00
	#2	Green "Clambroth," Hocking	75.00– 95.00
	#3	Green, unknown	30.00– 35.00
	#4	Refrigerator dish (sold as butter)	22.00– 25.00
Row 3:	**Hazel Atlas** tops embossed "BUTTER COVER"		
	#1	Green	50.00– 55.00
	#2	Crystal	22.00– 25.00
	#3	White	25.00– 30.00

Row 3:	(Continued)		
	#4	Cobalt blue	250.00–275.00
Row 4:	#1, 3	"Crisscross," 1 lb., green or pink	50.00– 55.00
	#2	Same, crystal	20.00– 25.00
	#4	Same, cobalt blue	95.00–110.00
Row 5:	#1, 3	Same, 1/4 lb., green or pink	35.00– 40.00
	#2	Same, crystal	15.00– 18.00
	#4	Same, cobalt blue	85.00– 95.00
Row 6:	#1	"Sanitary Refrigerator Jar"	150.00–165.00
	#2	Cheese, blue (foreign?)	125.00–140.00
	#3	"Hot & Cold" embossed	45.00– 50.00
	#4	Cheese "Sanitary Preserver"	35.00– 40.00

Page 95

Row 1:	#1	Fleur-de-lis pepper	6.00– 7.00
	#2	Fleur-de-lis salt	8.00–10.00
	#3-5	Fleur-de-lis coffee, sugar, flour, ea.	20.00–22.50
	#6	Large canister w/o label	4.00– 5.00
	#7	Small canister w/o label	1.00– 1.50
Row 2:	#1	Teal stacking jar set	25.00–30.00
	#2	Sugar shaker	20.00–22.00
	#3-7	Spice canisters (match canisters in Row 1), ea.	5.00– 6.00
	#8	Refrigerator container	5.00– 6.00
	#9	Teal canister	25.00–30.00
Row 3:	#1	Canister, 64 oz.	15.00–17.50

Row 3:	(Continued)		
	#2	Canister, 32 oz.	11.00–12.50
	#3-5	Canister, 8 oz., ea.	5.00– 6.00
	#6	Canister, 16 oz., "Three Bears"	12.50–15.00
Row 4:	#1,2	Canister white w/Mexican decal, ea.	10.00–12.50
	#3	Canister, 128 oz.	40.00–45.00
	#4	Hazel Atlas flour canister	25.00–30.00
Row 5:	#1	"Clambroth" white large canister	35.00–40.00
	#2	Same, medium	25.00–30.00
	#3	Same, small	15.00–17.50
	#4	L.E.Smith jar	50.00–55.00
	#5	L.E.Smith jar, larger version	60.00–65.00

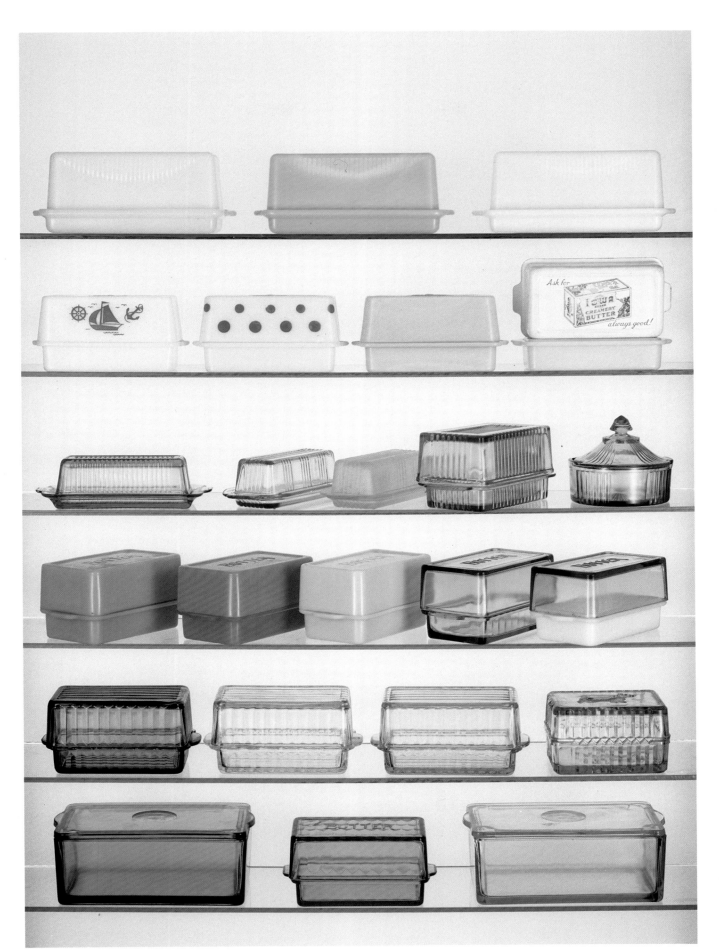

94

CRUETS and DISPENSERS (Refrigerator Type)

Page 97

Row 1: #1 Fostoria yellow "Trojan" 250.00–300.00
#2 Fostoria blue "Fairfax," w/stopper 150.00–200.00
#3 Fostoria amber "Fairfax," w/stopper 85.00–100.00
#4 Fostoria green "Mayfair" 100.00–125.00
#5 Same, yellow, w/stopper 100.00–125.00

Row 2: #1 Fostoria "Colony" 40.00– 45.00
#2 Fostoria yellow "Baroque," w/stopper 200.00–250.00
#3 Paden City pink #210 line 65.00– 75.00
#4 Same, green 65.00– 75.00
#5 Jadite "Vinegar" 200.00–250.00

Row 3: #1 U.S. Glass (?) set on tray 80.00– 90.00
#2 Imperial blue (not Heisey experimental blue) 75.00– 85.00
#3 Same as #1, pink 80.00– 90.00

Row 3: (Continued)
#4 Pink 50.00– 55.00

Row 4: #1 U.S. Glass green 40.00– 45.00
#2 Same, crystal 20.00– 22.00
#3 Same, pink 40.00– 45.00
#4 Imperial, pink 35.00– 40.00
#5 New Martinsville "Janice" blue 75.00– 85.00
#6 New Martinsville "Radiance" crystal 20.00– 25.00

Row 5: #1 Cambridge green 50.00– 55.00
#2 Same, amber 35.00– 40.00
#3 Cambridge, "Caprice" blue 70.00– 80.00
#4 Cambridge, "Apple Blossom" pink 125.00–150.00
#5 Cambridge, amber in Faberware 15.00– 20.00

Page 98

Row 1: #1 Imperial "Canary Yellow" (vaseline) 45.00– 50.00
#2 Imperial green 40.00– 45.00
#3 Imperial "Cape Cod" 22.00– 25.00
#4 Imperial ribbed & beaded, pink 40.00– 45.00
#5 Same, no beads 40.00– 45.00
#6 Heisey, crystal 30.00– 35.00

Row 2: #1 Lancaster Glass Company, yellow 60.00– 65.00
#2 Same, green 55.00– 65.00
#3 Pink blown (probably foreign) 40.00– 50.00
#4 Imperial pink 45.00– 50.00
#5 Fostoria "Garland" 50.00– 60.00
#6 Amber 30.00– 35.00

Row 3: #1 Heisey "Old Sandwich" w/stopper 85.00– 95.00
#2 Heisey "Yeoman" 50.00– 60.00
#3 Heisey "Twist," 4 oz., "Moongleam" green 75.00– 85.00

Row 3: (Continued)
#4 Same, "Flamingo" pink 75.00– 80.00
#5 Same, 2$^{1}\!/_{2}$ oz. 70.00– 75.00
#6 Imperial "Cape Cod" 15.00– 20.00
#7 Duncan "Caribbean" blue 75.00– 85.00

Row 4: #1 Duncan "Canterbury" 20.00– 25.00
#2 Red 100.00–120.00
#3 Green 40.00– 50.00
#4 Imperial's "Verde" green from Heisey "Crystolite" mold 15.00– 20.00
#5 Hazel Atlas green 40.00– 45.00
#6 Same, pink 50.00– 55.00

Row 5: #1, 2 U.S. Glass (?) dark green, ea. 35.00– 40.00
#3 Pink 30.00– 35.00
#4 Green 30.00– 35.00
#5 Crystal 18.00– 20.00
#6 Hocking green 30.00– 35.00

Page 99

Row 1: #1 L.E. Smith cobalt blue water dispenser 400.00–450.00
#2 Same, light blue 300.00–350.00
#3 McKee white dispenser 110.00–125.00

Row 2: #1 McKee Jade Green dispenser, 5$^{1}\!/_{4}$" tall 175.00–200.00
#2 McKee Jade Green dispenser 115.00–125.00

Row 2: (Continued)
#3 McKee custard dispenser 110.00–125.00

Row 3: #1 McKee w/Jade Green top 120.00–135.00
#2 Sneath Glass Co. green clambroth w/crystal top 75.00– 85.00
#3 Water dispenser, Jade Green top 55.00– 65.00

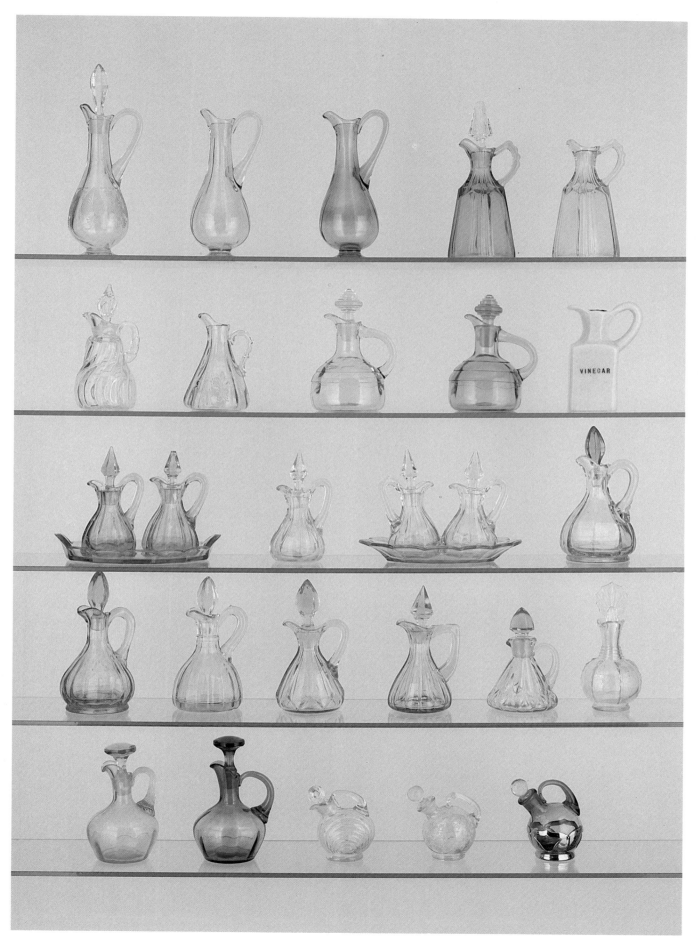

DISPENSERS, Drink and Juice

Antique shows that feature old advertising items are among the best places to find kitchenware collectibles. In days past, that was where I bought many of my colored straw holders as well as other kitchen related collectibles. Today, all that has changed is advertising dealers now attend Depression Glass shows to buy our Kitchenware to take to their shows. I miss the $150.00–200.00 prices for green straw jars at those shows!

The popularity of these remnants from restaurant and soda fountain days is awesome as my son used to say! Advertising shows draw collectors with megabucks. There are usually four or five of these dispensers at one of the larger shows. Rarely are there any unsold, if priced fairly, when it is over. One impediment, when it comes to exhibiting them, is size. Because of lingering nostalgic memories, most are finding homes on antique bars in the den or game room.

Page 101
Row 1:	#1	Crystal and Green (no name)	200.00–250.00
	#2	Samovar, green w/copper holder	200.00–225.00
Row 2:	#1	"Middleby" quality	150.00–175.00
	#2	"Orange Crush" type	175.00–200.00
	#3	Manufactured by E.B. Evans Co Philadelphia 33, Pa	200.00–225.00

Page 102
Row 1:	#1	Samovar yellow (possibly Paden City)	250.00–300.00
	#2	Mission Orange	300.00–350.00
	#3	Mission Grapefruit	325.00–350.00
Row 2:	#1	Paden City percolator, 3 piece, green	300.00–325.00
		Amber (not shown)	250.00–275.00
	#2	Mission Real Fruit Juice (pink)	175.00–200.00
	#3	Mission Real Fruit Juice (green)	175.00–200.00

Page 103
Row 1:	#1	Bireley's Orange Juice	350.00–375.00
	#2	Amber barrel and green base	275.00–300.00
	#3	Samovar green (possibly Paden City)	250.00–300.00
Row 2:	#1	Orange Crush	225.00–250.00

ICE BUCKETS & BEVERAGE DISPENSERS

The cobalt blue and amethyst beverage dispensers (top row of page 105) are Cambridge glass. Some have been found on a matching color round tray; but, so far, no sets have been found with any type of drinking vessel. They are marked on the bottom: "The American Thermos Bottle Co., Norwich, Conn. U.S.A.; Genuine Thermos Reg. U.S. Patent Office; Pat. App'd For: Vacuum Bottle." The metal bottle shown with these probably proved to be more durable!

Collectors of ice buckets tell me the first fifty buckets are found rather easily; the next fifty come with some difficulty; and once you have approximately one hundred, you can no longer find those you don't already own or the room to display them! I've seen photos of some super collections; and most of them have been very artfully displayed.

Page 105

Row 1:	#1	Cambridge cobalt blue	
		Thermos	350.00–400.00
	#2	Same, amethyst	300.00–350.00
	#3	Thermos	12.50– 15.00
	#4,	Ice box water bottle	12.50– 15.00
Row 2:	#1	Georgian ice bucket	35.00– 40.00
	#2	Ice bucket w/metal drainer	30.00– 35.00
	#3	Pink flared rim ice bucket	45.00– 50.00

Row 2: (Continued)

	#4	Pink elephant ice bucket	25.00– 30.00
	#5	Frosted and striped ice bucket	20.00– 25.00
Row 3:	#1	Metallic finish ice bucket	12.50– 15.00
	#2	Cambridge cobalt blue	
		ice bucket	100.00–125.00
	#3,5	Hocking Royal Ruby ribbed	
		or plain water w/lid, ea.	150.00–175.00
	#4	Black amethyst ice bucket	45.00– 50.00

Ice Buckets
Page 106

Row 1:	#1	Jeannette "Hex Optic"	
		w/reamer top, green	40.00–45.00
	#2	Van Deman "Black Forest,"	
		pink	60.00–65.00
	#3	Fostoria "Polar Bear"	30.00–35.00
	#4	McKee, green	20.00–25.00
Row 2:	#1	Fostoria "Swirl," blue	30.00–35.00
	#2	Fostoria "Colony"	85.00–95.00
	#3	Cambridge etched grapes	35.00–40.00
	#4	Fostoria, yellow	30.00–35.00
Row 3:	#1	Fostoria, pink	30.00–35.00
	#2	Fenton, jade	40.00–45.00
	#3	Same, black	40.00–50.00
	#4	Pink w/etched flower &	
		square bottom	25.00–30.00

Row 4:	#1	Cambridge, "Decagon,"	
		amethyst	35.00–40.00
	#2	Same, amber	30.00–35.00
	#3	Cambridge, green	30.00–35.00
	#4	Cambridge, #731 or	
		"Rosalie", blue	65.00–75.00
Row 5:	#1	Hocking "Frigidaire Ice	
		Server"	18.00–20.00
	#2	Hocking, "Ring"	18.00–20.00
	#3	Paden City (?) pink	22.00–25.00
	#4	Crystal, Made in U.S.A.	
		(English, other languages	
		on side)	12.00–15.00

Page 107

Row 1:	#1	Fry w/lid, pink	175.00–200.00
	#2	Same, green	200.00–225.00
	#3	Fenton, w/lid, yellow	115.00–135.00
	#4	Fenton, w/lid, jade	85.00–110.00
Row 2:	#1	Cambridge "Mt. Vernon,"	
		red	90.00–110.00
	#2	Fenton, w/lid, green	60.00– 75.00
	#3	Fenton "Plymouth," red	60.00– 75.00
	#4	Green w/metal lid	25.00– 35.00
Row 3:	#1	Pink "Diamond"	27.50– 35.00
	#2	Green "Zig-Zag"	25.00– 30.00
	#3	Green	20.00– 25.00

Row 3: (Continued)

	#4	Paden City "Party Line"	
		w/etched flowers, pink	25.00– 30.00
Row 4:	#1	Paden City "Party Line,"	
		pink	25.00– 30.00
	#2	Same, amber	25.00– 27.50
	#3, 4	Paden City "Cupid," green	
		or pink	200.00–250.00
Row 5:	#1	Paden City "Cupid" ice	
		tub, pink	200.00–225.00
	#2, 3	Paden City "Party Line"	
		ice tub, ea.	25.00– 30.00
	#4	Green ice tub	22.00– 25.00

KNIVES and LADLES

Knife prices have now stabilized. Most of the "comparable" colors are selling in the same price range. All the rarer knives are commanding higher prices!

Boxes add $3.00–5.00 to the price if in excellent condition. Boxes are placed near the knife found in that box. The box on the right in Row 1 of Page 109 says "New York World's Fair."

Page 111 ends the knives and starts the ladle section.

Some knives are priced and not shown.

Page 109

			Pink (lt/dk)	Blue	Crystal	Green
Row 1:	#1-3	3 Star, 8½"	25.00– 28.00	28.00– 30.00	8.00–10.00	
	#4-6	3 Star, 9¼"	25.00– 28.00	28.00– 30.00	8.00–10.00	
Row 2:	#1, 2	3 Leaf Dur-X, 8½"	25.00– 28.00	28.00– 30.00	8.00–10.00	25.00– 28.00
	#3, 4	3 Leaf, Dur-X, 9¼"	25.00– 28.00		10.00–12.00	
	#5	Same, (light amber)	125.00–150.00			
	#6-8	5 Leaf, Dur-X, 8½"		20.00– 25.00	10.00–12.00	20.00– 25.00

			Pink (lt/dk)	Amber	Crystal	Green
Row 3:	#1, 2	Rose spray, 8½"	*150.00–175.00	175.00–200.00	75.00–85.00	*150.00–175.00
	#3	Plain handle, 8½"			12.00–15.00	30.00– 35.00
	#4-6	Plain handle, 9¼"	30.00– 35.00			30.00– 35.00
	#7	Same, (pinkish/amber)	60.00– 75.00			

Page 110

			Pink (lt/dk)	Amber	Crystal	Green
Row 1:	#1-3	Block, 8¼"	30.00– 35.00		12.00– 15.00	22.50– 37.50
	#4-8	AER-FLO, 7½"	60.00– 70.00	200.00–225.00	30.00– 40.00	60.00– 70.00
	#9	Same, (Forest Green)	250.00–275.00			
Row 2:	#1-3	Steel-ite	80.00– 90.00		35.00– 45.00	80.00– 90.00
	#4	Stonex, 8¼", (white)	175.00–225.00			
	#5-8	Same, light or dark		175.00–195.00		50.00– 60.00
Row 3:	#1	Candlewick, 8½"			300.00–350.00	
	#2	Dagger, 9¼"			100.00–125.00	
	#3	Westmoreland, Thumb-guard, 9¼"			100.00–115.00	
	#4	Same, Flowers			20.00– 25.00	*300.00–350.00
	#5	Same, minature (sample?)			125.00–150.00	
	#6-8	Buffalo Knife (B.K.Co.), 9¼"			15.00– 18.00	35.00– 40.00

Page 111   Knives top to bottom upper left picture.

#1	Pinwheel	10.00– 12.00
#2,3	Plain	15.00– 18.00
#4-8	Colored handles/blades, ea.	25.00– 28.00

Ladles

Upper Right:

#1	White	35.00– 40.00
#2	"Radiance," blue	150.00–175.00
#3	White, Imperial	40.00– 45.00

Lower Left:

#1	Crystal	30.00– 35.00

Lower Left: (Continued)

#2	Black	110.00–125.00
#3	Crystal	25.00– 30.00
#4	Amber	25.00– 35.00

Lower Right:

#1	Duncan, "Caribbean"	40.00– 45.00
#2	Same, "Hobnail"	25.00– 30.00
#3, 4	Red handled	40.00– 50.00

*Not Shown

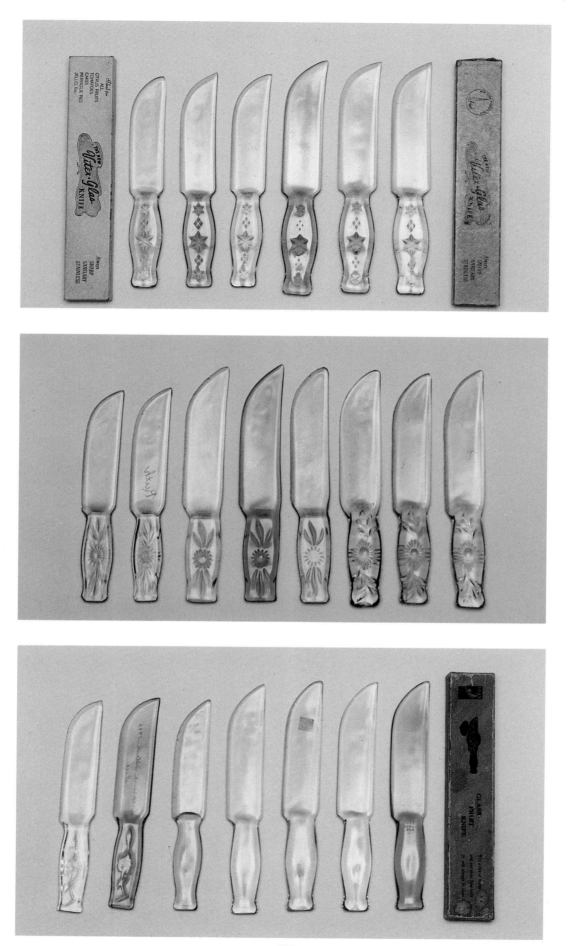

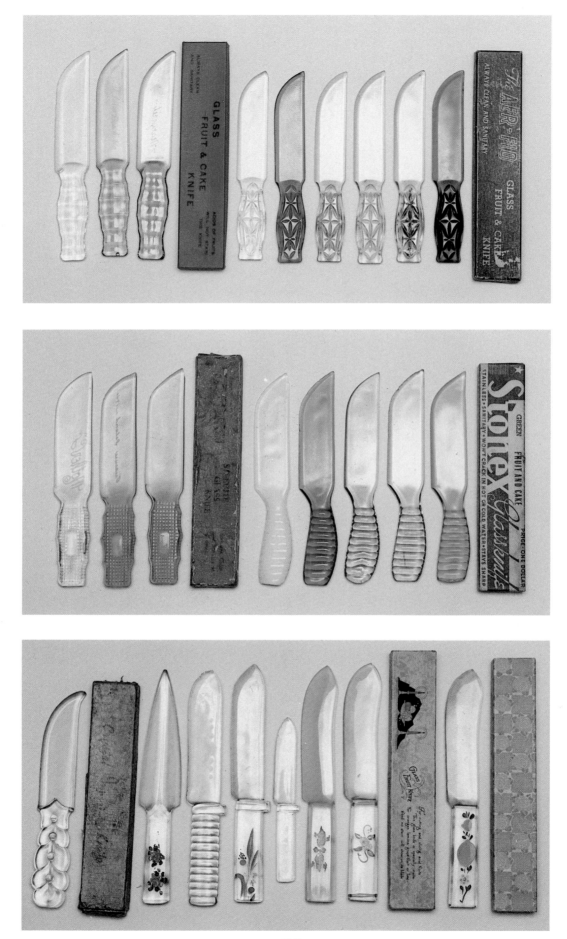

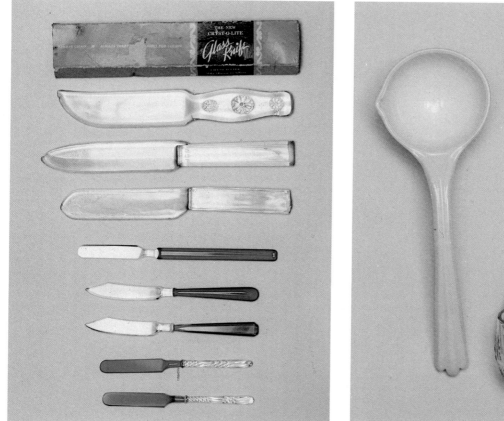 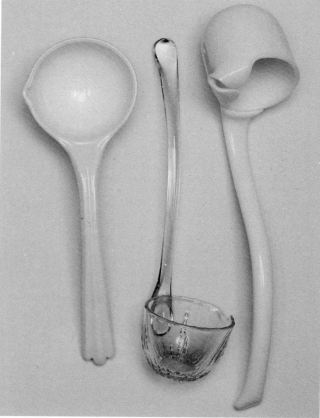

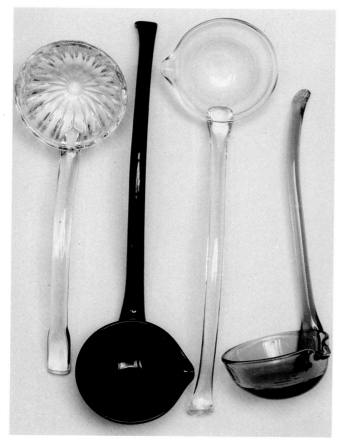 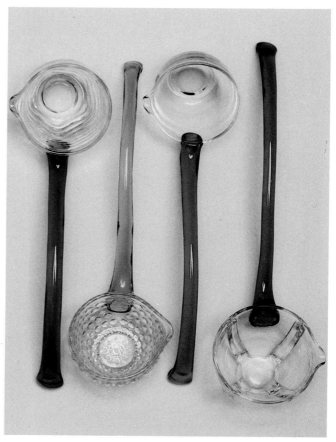

111

LADLES

Heisey, Fostoria, and Cambridge ladles are the most in demand, although other companies' ladles are collected. An abundance of black ladles with a dwindling demand for them has caused the price of those to plunge.

Page 113

Row 1:	#1	Duncan, "Festive"	20.00–22.00
	#2, 4	Pink	15.00–18.00
	#3, 5	Blue	22.00–25.00
Row 2:	#1	Cambridge, pink	20.00–25.00
	#2, 3	Same, green	20.00–25.00
	#4	Same, Forest Green	22.00–25.00
	#5	Same, Moonlight blue	40.00–45.00
	#6	Same, amber	20.00–25.00

Column 1:

	#1, 2	Green or yellow	15.00–18.00
	#3	Blue, criss crossing design	20.00–22.00
	#4, 5	Same, green or yellow	15.00–18.00

Column 2:

| | #1 | Fostoria, crystal | 12.00–15.00 |
| | #2 | Pink | 25.00–30.00 |

Column 2: (Continued)

	#3, 4	Same, yellow, amber, or *green	22.50–25.00
	#5	Same, light blue	40.00–45.00
	#6	Same, cobalt blue	40.00–45.00

Column 3:

	#1	Cambridge, blue	25.00–30.00
	#2-4	Same, green	20.00–22.00
	#5	Same, crystal	8.00–10.00

Column 4:

	#1	Cambridge, amberina	40.00–45.00
	#2	Same, Ivory	20.00–25.00
	#3	Same, Primrose	25.00–30.00
	#4	Same, Azurite	35.00–40.00
	#5	Ebony	25.00–30.00

Page 114

Row 1:	#1	Crystal, side spout	10.00–12.00
	#2-4	Candlewick, ea.	10.00–15.00
	#5	Higbee, signed bee in bottom	20.00–25.00
Row 2:	#1-4	Crystal, unusual shapes, ea.	8.00–10.00

Column 1 & 2: **All ladles have rounded bottoms.**

	#1 & 4-6	Crystal, plain & etched	8.00–10.00
	#2	Green	15.00–18.00
	#3	Black	25.00–30.00
	#7	Amethyst	25.00–30.00

Column 2:

| | #1, 2 & 4 | "Clambroth" green or blue | 20.00–25.00 |
| | #3 | Cobalt blue | 35.00–40.00 |

Column 2: (Continued)

| | #5, 6 | Pink or amber | 22.00–25.00 |
| | #7 | Black | 25.00–30.00 |

Column 3: **All ladles have wedge shaped handles.**

	#1 & 10	White	12.00–15.00
	#2	Black	25.00–30.00
	#3, 4 & 8	Blue, ea.	18.00–22.00
	#5	Crystal	8.00–10.00
	#6, 7 & 9	Yellow, pink or green	15.00–18.00

Column 4: **All ladles have rounded handles.**

	#1, 8	Forest green, light blue	15.00–18.00
	#2, 5 & 10	Crystal, ea.	8.00–10.00
	#3, 4 & 6	Pink or green	15.00–18.00
	#7	Amber	12.00–15.00
	#9	Black	25.00–30.00

Page 115

Row 1:	#1-3	All iridized carnival colors	30.00–35.00
Row 2:	#1,2	Heisey, Flamingo, ea.	25.00–30.00
	#3,4	Same, Hawthorne	30.00–35.00
	#5	Same, Moongleam	30.00–35.00

Columns 1 & 2: **All ladles have flat bottoms.**

Column 1:

	#1, 5	Flashed or amber	8.00–10.00
	#2, 4, 6, 7	Yellow, green or pink	15.00–18.00
	#3	Blue	20.00–25.00
	#8	Cobalt blue, etched	35.00–40.00

Column 2:

| | #1 | Cobalt blue | 35.00–40.00 |
| | #2 | Amethyst | 25.00–28.00 |

Column 2: (Continued)

	#3	Amber	12.00–15.00
	#4, 6	Frosted blue or vaseline	20.00–25.00
	#5	Crystal	8.00–10.00

Column 3: **All ladle knobs end in triangle shape.**

	#1	Amber	12.00–15.00
	#2	Green	15.00–18.00
	#3, 5	Amethyst or vaseline	20.00–25.00
	#4	Red	35.00–40.00

Column 4: **All ladle knobs end in straight line.**

	#1	Red	35.00–40.00
	#2, 4	Frosted & vaseline	25.00–30.00
	#3, 6	Flashed or amber	10.00–12.00
	#5	Green	15.00–18.00

*Not Shown

113

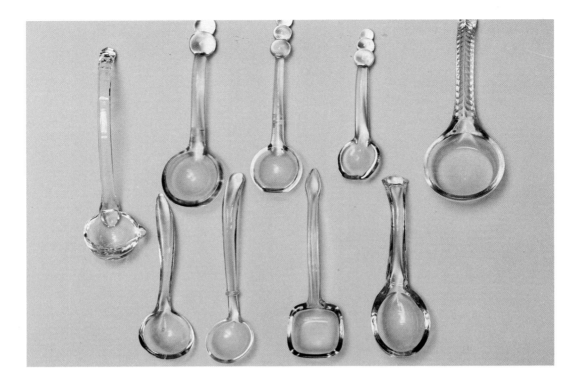

MEASURING CUPS, Advertising & Pattern Glass

Advertising measuring cup prices vary greatly. Dealers who specialize in advertising items seem to value these cups more highly than do measuring cup collectors. Many advertising dealers feel that any cup, including the later Fire King cups with ads, are worth at least $20.00. Some are, but not all! Only two people can decide the price – the buyer and the seller.

There are not many pattern glass measuring cups on the market, but those with lids are harder to find. Lids are interchangeable on many of these cups.

Row 1:	#1, 4, 5	Westmoreland w/measure lid (most have advertising in base such as "Finley Acker & Co.," highest grade at lowest cost	75.00– 85.00
		w/o measure lid	35.00– 40.00
	#2, 3	Measurements below spout; w/o measure lid $60.00–65.00; w/lid	90.00–100.00
Row 2:	#1-4	All Westmoreland w/ads, ea.	20.00– 25.00
		"USE SILAS PIERCE PURE SPICE"	
		"USE SHEPARD'S DRAWING ROOM TEA"	
		"USE S.S.SLEEPER'S, Best of all Spices"	
		"USE GILLESPIE'S ORIENTAL FLOUR"	
	#5	"ARCADE MFG. & CO., Freeport, Ill"	20.00– 25.00
Row 3:	#1	"SELLER'S," Pat. Dec. 8, 1925	25.00– 30.00
	#2	"J W POFF & SONS," Wrightsville, Pa.	20.00– 25.00
	#3	"NAPANEE" Dutch Kitchen Cabinet, world's finest kitchen cabinets, Coppes Bros. & Zook, Napanee, IN	20.00– 30.00
	#4	"PICKERINGS," Your credit is good, complete home furnishings, 10th & Penn, Pittsburgh	20.00– 30.00
	#5	"OWENS & CO."	20.00– 30.00
Row 4:	#1	"SILVERS," Brooklyn, Trademark (picture Brooklyn Bridge)	20.00– 30.00
	#2	"SAGINAW MILLING CO."	20.00– 30.00
	#3	"BUNKER HILL COFFEE"	20.00– 30.00
	#4	"CLOVERDALE" quality (4 leaf clover in red)	20.00– 30.00
	#5	"CAPITAL B BAND" Handy Cup Measure	25.00– 30.00
Row 5:	#1	"TIPPE CANOE," Kitchen Cabinets, none better	20.00– 30.00
	#2	"KEYSTONE FURN. CO.," The store that charges less, W King St., Lancaster, Pa.	20.00– 25.00
	#3	"HEALTH CLUB" Baking Powder for Success in every baking	20.00– 30.00
	#4	"STICKNEY & POOR" Boston Spice Co.	20.00– 30.00
	#5	"STICKNEY & POOR" Spice Co.	20.00– 30.00
Row 6:	#1	"SCOUT CABIN"	20.00– 25.00
	#2	"BROWN EKBERG" Golden Rule Store	20.00– 30.00
	#3	"ARMOUR," Use Armour's extract of beef	20.00– 25.00
	#4	"FLUFFO," "Be sure of success, use Fluffo shortening & salad oil"	20.00– 25.00
	#5	"CREAM DOVE" Brand Peanut Butter Salad Dressing, Cream Dove Mfg. in Binghamton, NY	20.00– 30.00

MEASURING CUPS, Jeannette, McKee, Federal, Hazel Atlas, Anchor Hocking, etc.

See Reproduction Section pages 236-237 for items with asterisk.

Page 119

Rows 1-3: **Jeannette Sets** except *Row 3:* Green $25.00–28.00; Pink $25.00–28.00

	Ultra-marine	Pink	Crystal	Delphite	Jadite
1 cup	50.00– 55.00	55.00– 60.00	40.00– 45.00	50.00– 55.00	22.00–25.00
1/2 cup	40.00– 45.00	50.00– 55.00	40.00– 45.00	45.00– 50.00	20.00–22.00
1/3 cup	35.00– 40.00	50.00– 55.00	35.00– 40.00	45.00– 50.00	20.00–22.00
1/4 cup	25.00– 30.00	40.00– 45.00	35.00– 40.00	35.00– 40.00	15.00–18.00
Set	150.00–170.00	195.00–215.00	150.00–170.00	175.00–195.00	77.00–87.00

Row 4:
- #1 McKee unembossed Glasbake, stippled bottom — 18.00–20.00
- #2 McKee Glasbake, fired-on red — 25.00–30.00
- #3 Glasbake, embossed — 18.00–20.00
- #4 Same, white — 45.00–50.00
- #5 Same, white w/red trim — 45.00–50.00

Row 5:
- #1, 2 Same, handle variations — 12.00–15.00
- #3 Radnt, 2 spout — 70.00–80.00
- #4 Glasbake (A.J. Novite & Sons; Charleston, 3 S.C.) — 15.00–20.00

Row 6:

Chalaine Blue	Black	Seville Yellow	Jadite	Crystal	Caramel
700.00–800.00	700.00–800.00	175.00–195.00	175.00–195.00	65.00–75.00	500.00–600.00

Page 120

Row 1:
- #1 Federal grn., w/o hdl., 3 spt. — 30.00–35.00
- #2 Same, crystal — 18.00–20.00
- #3 Same, amber — 35.00–38.00
- #4 Same, 3 spout, handle ad: "Easy Combomatic Washer/Dryer" — 22.50–25.00
- #5 Same, pink — 55.00–60.00
- #6 Same, amber — 35.00–38.00

Row 2:
- #1, 3 Same, solid hdl, 1 or 3 spt. — 40.00–45.00
- #2 Same, crystal — 22.50–25.00
- #4 Fry, 3 spout — 65.00–75.00
- #5 Same, 1 spout — 60.00–70.00

Row 3:
- #1-3 Hazel Atlas 3 spt white/trim — 55.00–65.00
- #4 Same, flashed green — 32.00–35.00
- #5, 6 Same, white or flashed red — 35.00–40.00

Row 4: #1, 2 Hazel Atlas 1 or 3 spout,
- green — 25.00– 30.00
- #3, 4 Same, pink, no embossing — 35.00– 38.00
- #5 Same, crystal — 15.00– 18.00

Row 5:
- #1 Hazel Atlas 3 spout, yellow — 250.00–285.00
- #2 Same, cobalt blue — *350.00–400.00
- #3 Green, HA embosssed — 25.00– 30.00
- #4 Kellogg's embossed, pink — *30.00– 35.00
- #5 Kellogg's embossed, green — *30.00– 35.00

Row 6:
- #1 Cambridge, crystal — 20.00– 25.00
- #2 Heisey, crystal — 250.00–285.00
- #3, 4 Foreign, ea. — 18.00– 20.00
- #5 Blue foreign, EJKRONT (measures tea, coffee, wine) — 45.00– 50.00
- #6 Cobalt blue, foreign "SEPDELEN" — 75.00– 85.00

Page 121

Row 1:
- #1 Fire King, blue 3 spout — 22.00– 25.00
- #2 Fire King, blue 1 spout — 20.00– 22.00
- #3 Fire King, crystal w/red — 3.00– 5.00
- #4 Gr. emb "Urban's Liberty Flour" — 65.00– 75.00
- #5 Pyrex, 2 spout — 22.00– 25.00
- #6 Pyrex, 1 spout — 12.00– 15.00

Row 2:
- #1, 2 Green "Clambroth," ea. — 175.00–200.00
- #3-5 Hocking green, ea. — 30.00– 35.00
- #6 Hocking crystal — 15.00– 18.00

Row 3:
- #1 Gr. slick hdl., dry measure "Sellers" — 50.00– 60.00
- #2 Same, "E.E. Hamm," Hanover, Pa. — 35.00– 40.00
- #3, 5 U.S. Glass slick, hdl., 2 spout, ea. — 35.00– 40.00
- #4 Same, green, 1 spout — 35.00– 40.00
- #6 Crystal, dry measure — 15.00– 20.00

Row 4:
- #1 U.S. Glass pink, 1 spout — 50.00– 60.00
- #2, 3 U.S. Glass, green 1 or 3 spout — 30.00– 35.00

Row 4: (Continued)
- #4 Spoon measure — 12.00– 15.00
- #5 U.S. Glass, dry measure, white — 175.00–200.00
- #6 Paden City, green — 125.00–145.00

Row 5:
- #1 Green 3 spout — 75.00– 85.00
- #2 Crystal, oval — 15.00– 20.00
- #3 Same, green — 55.00– 65.00
- #4 Tufglas — 85.00–100.00
- #5, 6 Crystal, (rnd bot) or "Ideal" measure — 25.00– 30.00

Row 6:
- #1 Green, 1 spout — 75.00– 85.00
- #2, 4, 5 Crystal, 1 spt, or rectangular, ea. — 20.00– 22.00
- #3 Amber, 1 spout — 250.00–275.00
- #6 Amber — 25.00– 30.00
- #7, 8 Crystal "Root Tea"/"My Pet Milk" — 20.00– 25.00

MEASURING CUPS, Rare and Unusual

There are some difficult to find measuring cups shown here. The footed four cup pitchers in Delphite and "Caramel" are the only ones ever found in those colors. I reiterate from the last book that, "Pricing unique pieces is at best, a guess."

It is difficult to obtain an accurate price on items that have not been sold in years. For example, a Chalaine blue four cup measure without handles was bought for $100.00 in 1980. One of these just sold for $1500.00 in Colorado. Is the only other one known worth the same – or more? How many collectors are willing to pay that much for the privilege of owning a Chalaine blue four cup measure?

Row 1:	#1	Chalaine Blue, 4 cup, no handle	1,250.00–1,500.00
	#2	Same, Seville yellow	400.00– 450.00
	#3	Same, Jadite green	400.00– 450.00
	#4	Same, crystal	100.00– 115.00
	#5	Tufglas, 4 cup	65.00– 70.00
Row 2:	#1	Seville yellow, 4 cup, ftd. w/hdl	115.00– 130.00
	#2	Same, Chalaine blue	400.00– 450.00
	#3	Same, Jadite	30.00– 35.00
	#4	Same, Custard	30.00– 35.00
Row 3:	#1	Cambridge dry measure, green	250.00– 275.00
	#2	Cambridge, 1 spout, 1 cup, pink	225.00– 250.00
	#3	Same, green	225.00– 250.00
	#4	U.S. Glass, 2 cup, pink	175.00– 195.00
Row 4:	#1	McKee, 4 cup, Caramel	500.00– 600.00
	#2	Same, Delphite	500.00– 550.00
	#3	Unknown, green, 2 cups = 1 pt. & 20 oz. = 1 pt. on side	125.00– 150.00

MEASURING CUP

1C778—8 oz., 3 in. high, heavy crystal, well finished, graduated for cups. 4 doz. in carton, 48 lbs. . . . .**Doz 48c**

GLASS MEASURING CUPS

No. 3   No. 2

No. 3—Half Pint Glass Measuring Cup. Packed 2 dozen to carton.
Per dozen $1.56
No. 2—Half Pint Glass Measuring Cup. Packed 2 dozen to carton.
Per dozen $2.20

MEASURING CUPS

Emerald Green

1C2193 — 8 oz., 3 in. high, clear crystal, lipped, graduated for ounces and pints. 2 doz. in carton, 30 lbs. . . . .**Doz 78c**

1C779—8 oz., 3⅛ in. high, substantial pressed **emerald green** glass, graduated for ounces and cups. 2 doz. in carton, 25 lbs. **Doz 85c**

1C2183—2 styles, plain and side lip, 8 oz., 3¼ in. high, clear crystal, graduated for ounces and cups. Asstd. 3 doz. in carton. **Doz 79c**

MEASURING CUPS CO-734 — · 2 doz in carton, 18 lbs
Doz 78c
8 oz., 3⅝ in., pressed cup and ounce graduated.

MEASURING PITCHERS, 2 Cups or More

Nearly all the measuring pitchers are bought by reamer collectors looking for bottoms to go with their reamer tops or hoping to find tops to the pitcher later. There are some rarities in these pitchers. Take note of the green one in Row 2 on page 127. It is probably the most desirable on these three pages.

There are more measuring cup collectors than there are measuring pitcher collectors. Owning decorated McKee two cup pitchers alone could fill several shelves in your china cabinet! Just take a look at the top three rows on Page 125. Considering that each of those designs could come on white or Custard as well as all the different colors gives an idea how many reamer tops you would need to complete these sets. **See Reproduction Section pages 236 – 237 for items marked with asterisk (*).**

Page 125

Rows 1-4		**All McKee 2 Cup**	
Row 1:	#1, 2	"Diamond Check," red or black	30.00–35.00
	#3	Floral decal	30.00–35.00
	#4, 5	Green or red "Dots" on white	28.00–32.00
Row 2:	#1-3	Floral, black or red bows, ea.	28.00–32.00
	#4, 5	"Ships"	30.00–35.00
Row 3:	#1, 2	Black or orange "Dots" on custard	35.00–38.00
	#3	Custard w/red trim	20.00–22.00
	#4	Custard	18.00–20.00
	#5	Seville yellow	35.00–38.00
Row 4:	#1	Jadite	20.00–22.00
	#2	Delphite	75.00–85.00

Row 4:		(Continued)	
	#3	Fired-on green	12.00–15.00
	#4	Glasbake, crystal	22.00–25.00
Row 5:	#1, 2	U.S.Glass, slick handle, pink or green	40.00–45.00
	#3	Same, crystal	18.00–20.00
	#4	Iridized carnival	35.00–45.00
	#5	Crystal	10.00–12.00
Row 6:		**All Jeannette 2 Cup (Sunflower in bottom)**	
	#1	Green transparent	85.00–95.00
	#2	Jadite, dark	45.00–450.00
	#3	Jadite, light	20.00–22.00
	#4	Delphite	70.00–80.00

Page 126

Row 1:	#1	Hocking, 2 cup, green	20.00– 25.00
	#2	Same, ribbed, green	45.00– 50.00
	#3	Same, crystal	20.00– 22.00
	#4	Same, pink	50.00– 55.00
Row 2:	#1	Green "Clambroth"	125.00–145.00
	#2	Vitrock white w/lid	30.00– 40.00
	#3	Fire-King, 16 oz., 2 spout, blue	25.00– 28.00
		Same, crystal embossed "Diamond Crystal Shaker Salt"	20.00– 25.00
	#4	"Grandma's Old Time Measure," made in Italy, 1971	18.00– 20.00
Row 3:	#1	Embossed "A & J"	12.00– 15.00
		Hazel Atlas (Measuring & Mixing in base)	
	#2	Fired-on red	35.00– 40.00

Row 3:		(Continued)	
	#3, 4	White w/decorated colored bands	25.00– 30.00
Row 4:	#1, 3 & 4	White w/Dots	35.00– 40.00
	#2	Green w/white Dots	40.00– 45.00
	#5	Black floral decal	30.00– 35.00
Row 5:	#1	Iridized	85.00–100.00
	#2	Transparent green	25.00– 30.00
	#3	Crystal	10.00– 15.00
	#4	Crystal, "Spry"	15.00– 18.00
Row 6:	#1	Cobalt blue	*195.00–220.00
	#2	Pink, light	*55.00– 65.00
	#3	Pink, dark	*110.00–125.00
	#4	Yellow	225.00–250.00

Page 127

Row 1:	#1	"Ocean Mills," Montreal, Canada (Man holding box of Chinese starch), 2$\frac{1}{2}$ pt.	60.00– 75.00
	#2	"Davis Baking Powder," $\frac{1}{2}$ gal.	60.00– 75.00
	#3	$\frac{1}{2}$ gal.	40.00– 50.00
Row 2:	#1	1 qt.	40.00– 45.00
	#2	1 qt., green	700.00–750.00
	#3	Cambridge, 1 qt., measure top	85.00–100.00
	#4	Baby formula, 20 oz., (foreign) Estans Materna	25.00– 30.00
Row 3:	#1	Umpire Glass Co., Pittsburgh, 1 qt.	25.00– 30.00

Row 3:		(Continued)	
	#2	Silvers Brooklyn Trademark, 1 qt.	25.00– 30.00
	#3	Sanitary Bess Mixer (embossed "4" inside a large "1")	175.00–200.00
	#4	Lighting Dasher Egg Beater Co., 1 pt.	20.00– 25.00
	#5	Hazel Atlas 4 cup crystal	20.00– 22.00
Row 4:	#1	Hazel Atlas frosted green	25.00– 30.00
	#2	White w/red trim, ea.	*20.00– 22.00
	#3	Hazel Atlas A&J green	25.00– 30.00
	#4	White w/black trim	20.00– 25.00

MECHANICAL ATTACHMENTS

Shown on the right below and in the middle of Row 3 on page 129 are two different "Cold Water Coffee Extractors." Neither of these were ever used so they may have been a great idea that wasn't popular. Instructions for use are shown on page 130. Additionally, instructions for the "Economy Dispenser" pictured below on the left are shown on page 131.

Page 128
Row 1:   #1   Filtron cold water coffee extractor   125.00–150.00
            #2   Economy dispenser   50.00– 60.00

Page 129
Row 1:   #1   Mayonnaise maker   12.50– 15.00
            #2   Sugar shaker (one tsp. measure top)   40.00– 45.00
            #3   Honey or other liquid dispenser   15.00– 17.50
            #4   Syrup dispenser   12.50– 15.00
            #5   "Vidrio" electric mixer w/green base   50.00– 60.00
Row 2:   #1   Mixer   10.00– 15.00
            #2   Food chopper   15.00– 18.00
            #3   Mixer   12.00– 15.00
            #4   Mixer, bands at 4-8-12 oz. marks   12.00– 15.00
            #5   Electric beater   20.00– 25.00
Row 3:   #1   Mixer   20.00– 25.00
            #2   Measure for CoffeeX coffee extractor   12.50– 15.00
            #3   CoffeeX cold water coffee extractor   125.00–150.00
            #4   Green butter churn   325.00–350.00

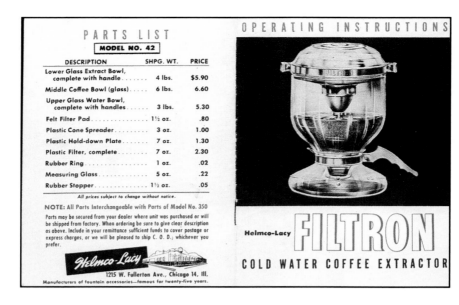

PARTS LIST

MODEL NO. 42

DESCRIPTION	SHPG. WT.	PRICE
Lower Glass Extract Bowl, complete with handle	4 lbs.	$5.90
Middle Coffee Bowl (glass)	6 lbs.	6.60
Upper Glass Water Bowl, complete with handles	3 lbs.	5.30
Felt Filter Pad	1½ oz.	.80
Plastic Cone Spreader	3 oz.	1.00
Plastic Hold-down Plate	7 oz.	1.30
Plastic Filter, complete	7 oz.	2.30
Rubber Ring	1 oz.	.02
Measuring Glass	5 oz.	.22
Rubber Stopper	1½ oz.	.05

All prices subject to change without notice.

NOTE: All Parts Interchangeable with Parts of Model No. 350

Parts may be secured from your dealer where unit was purchased or will be shipped from factory. When ordering be sure to give clear description as above. Include in your remittance sufficient funds to cover postage or express charges, or we will be pleased to ship C. O. D.; whichever you prefer.

Helmco-Lacy

1215 W. Fullerton Ave., Chicago 14, Ill.
Manufacturers of fountain accessories—famous for twenty-five years.

OPERATING INSTRUCTIONS

Helmco-Lacy FILTRON
COLD WATER COFFEE EXTRACTOR

CARE OF NEW UNIT

Rinse the parts of your new Filtron thoroughly with cold drinking water—*do not use soap*—to remove the dust. Nothing else is necessary before starting the following simple instructions.

INSTRUCTIONS FOR OPERATING

- Fill water bowl with 60 oz. of clear, cold drinking water.
- Flush cold drinking water through plastic filter.
- Screw filter on water bowl so it cushions gently against rubber ring. (Use slight pressure of fingers only.)
- Insert rubber stopper in coffee bowl from **bottom**.
- Saturate felt pad **thoroughly**, cup slightly, and place in position, tab up.

It's as simple as A-B-C to operate — it requires less than two minutes to assemble your new Filtron if you follow the simple instructions. Then with Filtron extract always in your refrigerator you will have the most delicious cup of coffee you ever tasted — ready at an instant's notice. Follow these instructions and your Filtron will give you long, treasured service.

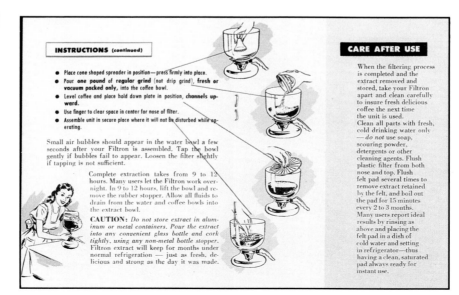

INSTRUCTIONS (continued)

- Place cone shaped spreader in position—press firmly into place.
- Pour **one pound of regular grind** (not drip grind), **fresh or vacuum packed only**, into the coffee bowl.
- Level coffee and place hold down plate in position, **channels upward**.
- Use finger to clear space in center for nose of filter.
- Assemble unit in secure place where it will not be disturbed while operating.

Small air bubbles should appear in the water bowl a few seconds after your Filtron is assembled. Tap the bowl gently if bubbles fail to appear. Loosen the filter slightly if tapping is not sufficient.

Complete extraction takes from 9 to 12 hours. Many users let the Filtron work overnight. In 9 to 12 hours, lift the bowl and remove the rubber stopper. Allow all fluids to drain from the water and coffee bowls into the extract bowl.

CAUTION: *Do not store extract in aluminum or metal containers. Pour the extract into any convenient glass bottle and cork tightly, using any non-metal bottle stopper.* Filtron extract will keep for months under normal refrigeration — just as fresh, delicious and strong as the day it was made.

CARE AFTER USE

When the filtering process is completed and the extract removed and stored, take your Filtron apart and clean carefully to insure fresh delicious coffee the next time the unit is used. Clean all parts with fresh, cold drinking water only — *do not* use soap, scouring powder, detergents or other cleaning agents. Flush plastic filter from both nose and top. Flush felt pad several times to remove extract retained by the felt, and boil out the pad for 15 minutes every 2 to 3 months. Many users report ideal results by rinsing as above and placing the felt pad in a dish of cold water and setting in refrigerator—thus having a clean, saturated pad always ready for instant use.

Directions for Installing and Use

USE THE screws provided and fasten the lock-band to the wall, cupboard-end, window or door casing or wherever desired. Fill glass container with coffee, or other commodity, then screw dispensing mechanism to container and turn upside-down with handle pointing downward. Now slip dispenser down through the lock-band and close dispensing mechanism by throwing handle up as far as it will go. The device is now ready for dispensing. NOTE: the handle will not slip through the lock-band unless the gate on the outer end of the measuring tube is open. This household model (No. 44) dispenses one rounded tablespoonful at a time. Always operate the handle through its full stroke for full measurements.

Economy Dispensers

IDEAL FOR MANY PURPOSES

ECONOMY DISPENSERS are now being used for a great many purposes. In the home for coffee, powdered, granulated, chip and flake soaps, tea, and other uses; in the laundry and in the bath for powdered toilet soaps and bath salts.

Soda fountains use a special model, with a standard for the back bar, or a bracket for attaching to the front bar, for dispensing malted milk, Ovaltine, Bromo-Seltzer, ground and flaked nuts, etc. Sanitary service the same to every customer.

Special Dispensers Designed for All Purposes Submit Your Problems

Economy Dispenser Corporation

648 Santa Fe Avenue
LOS ANGELES, CAL.

A New Invention

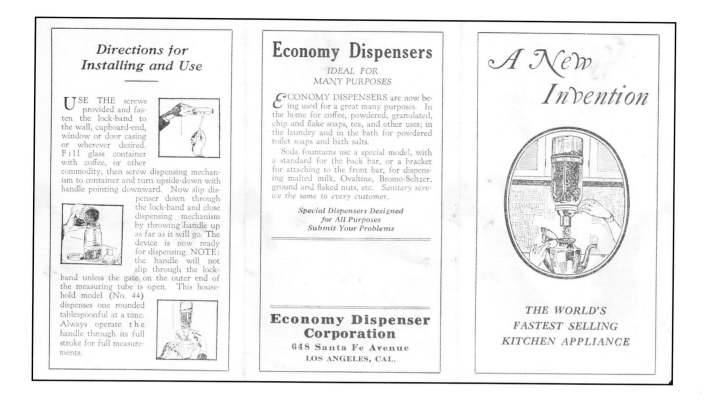

THE WORLD'S FASTEST SELLING KITCHEN APPLIANCE

MODEL NO. 44

For All Household Uses

Housewives are using this new device to simplify and make easier their housework for it is found to save many steps—much time and trouble.

The glass container shows just how much coffee, tea, soap, etc., is on hand. The contents are kept fresh and moisture-proof and are automatically dispensed in exact measured quantities.

Convenient and Economical

No more getting out the coffee can and finding it empty; no more looking for a spoon to measure with; no more coffee spilled on the drain board. And as a soap dispenser! No more reaching under the sink for the box of soap and guessing at the quantity to use. This dispenser will save the average family $5.00 a year and last a life-time.

Household Model Price $2.00

Fountain Models $5.00

It's Easy To Make Good Coffee Now

Time and again you have opened a fresh can of coffee—doesn't the aroma just seem to rise up and hit you in the face? But you have never had this experience when re-opening the can after the coffee has been about all used. Deterioration of strength and aroma begins the moment the can is opened. Each time it is opened thereafter the coffee becomes weaker and the last coffee from the can never was nor never will be the same delicious flavor as the first. The Economy Dispenser absolutely keeps coffee 100% perfect because it keeps it air-tight. There is no waste and the measurement is always the same.

A Beautiful Appearance

The Economy Dispenser is often spoken of as the best looking device in the kitchen. Made of crystal-clear glass with its locking band and dispensing mechanism of highly polished nickel it is really a beautiful addition to any kitchen. Every housewife is proud to have and finds satisfaction in using the Economy Dispensers. In some homes you will find from two to half a dozen in constant use.

131

MECHANICAL ATTACHMENTS (Continued)

I recently received a letter from a reader requesting instructions on how to work the two ice cream makers. These sanitary freezers, as they were called, are shown in the middle of Row 1 on page 133 and on the end of Row 1 on page 134. The instructions for operating the one on page 133 were in it, but I did not take them out to see how it was done. I suspect they were the "Ronco" of the radio age. You probably stir, put in ice box, stir later and put back in ice box, hoping not to blow up the glass container.

These accessory items make up some of the more unusual items in Kitchenware collecting. For those who collect colors, there are mechanical or hand beaters in almost every color. If you collect Fire King, there is a popcorn maker.

A one quart ice cream maker is shown at the bottom of page 134. An ice cube breaker is attached right beside it. I thought this was a great idea, but it was the first I had seen; so it may not have been too popular! I do know how to make this one work! I have done that chore! This is quite heavy; we had to triple the glass shelves to hold the mixer and the ice cream maker.

Page 133

Row 1: #1   "Keystone" beater, Pat. Dec. 1885, North Bros.   75.00– 85.00
     #2   Jewel "Beater Mixer" (mfg. by Juergens Bros., Minn., Mn.) 45.00– 50.00
     #3   Sanitary glass ice cream freezer (Consolidated Mfg. Co.)   75.00– 90.00
     #4   Mixer, 1 qt. capacity   15.00– 18.00
     #5   "Ladd" beater, green or pink (not shown)   35.00– 38.00
Row 2: #1   Hydraulic "Niagara" food mixer (attaches to faucet)   30.00– 35.00
     #2   Thermos (mercury lined), "Higbee Hot/Cold Sanitary Bottle"   75.00– 85.00

Row 2: (Continued)
     #3   Criss Cross food mixer (baby face on side)   55.00– 65.00
     #4   Mixer, bands at 4-8-12 oz. marks, Kamkap, Inc., U.S.A. 12.00– 15.00
     #5   Fire-King popcorn popper   35.00– 40.00
Row 3: #1   "Vidrio" electric mixer w/ cobalt blue base   125.00–135.00
     #2   Same, w/custard slag base   50.00– 55.00
     #3   "Chicago Electric" beater w/ Jadite bottom   40.00– 45.00
     #4   "Challenge" w/Custard bottom   30.00– 35.00
     #5   "Kenmore" electric beater   20.00– 25.00

Page 134

Row 1: #1   Delphite beater bowl   70.00– 75.00
     #2   Jadite beater bowl   30.00– 35.00
     #3   White beater bowl   20.00– 25.00
     #4   Iridized beater bowl   35.00– 40.00
     #5   Sanitary freezer   60.00– 75.00
Row 2: #1   Handy Andy Juice Extractor 30.00– 35.00
     #2   Juice extractor   100.00–125.00
     #3   Ser-Mor Juice Extractor Pat. 50.00– 60.00

Row 2: (Continued)
     #4   Vidrio Products Corp. "Gem Squeezer" Cicero, Il. 40.00– 50.00
Row 3: #1   Mixer, w/Chalaine bowl   100.00–125.00
     #2   "Deluxe Lightning One Quart Ice Cream Maker" w/Lightning Ice Cube Breaker by North Brothers   65.00–100.00

Page 135

Row 1: #1   "J. Hutchanson" Trademark S&S Long Island (Mayonnaise) 100.00– 125.00
     #2   Cobalt beater   100.00– 125.00
     #3   Ultra-marine beater   50.00– 55.00
     #4   Pink beater   30.00– 35.00
Row 2: #1   "Bromo-Seltzer" dispenser 135.00–150.00
     #2   "Ladd" mixer churn #2   85.00–100.00
     #3   Mixer (similar to Keystone) 75.00– 80.00
     #4   "Silver & Co." food mixer   20.00– 25.00
     #5   "Bordens" Pat. Mar. 30, 1915 18.00– 22.00

MISCELLANEOUS and MIXERS

Every time you have a large photography session for a book, there are items that do not go in the categories you are presently working on. Also, there are times that a quantity of harder to find items are available to be photographed when you are not even working on a book at the time. That is how pages 137 and 138 came to be. On page 139 are two complete mixers. The insert in the top of the mixer is impossible to find. Separately, that piece is worth more than the rest of the mixer. The mechanical parts of these mixers are worth very little. Their being glass makes them collectable.

Page 137

Row 1:	#1	Fry covered jug	175.00– 195.00
	#2	Unusual Fry pitcher	150.00– 165.00
	#3	Paden City cobalt blue sugar shaker	900.00– 950.00
Row 2:	#1	Green sugar shaker	175.00– 195.00
	#2	Pink sugar shaker	200.00– 225.00
	#3	Cobalt blue 3 ftd. sugar shaker (New Martinsville)?	750.00– 850.00
	#3,4	Green door knobs, pr.	125.00– 135.00
	#5,6	Cobalt blue door knobs, pr.	150.00– 200.00
Row 3:	#1	"Paramount" napkin holder, black	450.00– 495.00
	#2	Same, pink	425.00– 450.00
	#3	Candlewick knife	250.00– 275.00
Row 4:	#1	Hocking "Mayfair blue" reamer	1250.00–1500.00
	#2	Teal measure cup	200.00– 225.00
	#3	Salad set, cobalt blue	250.00– 300.00

Page 138

Row 1:	#1,5	Hocking batter dispenser	20.00– 25.00
	#2,4	Syrup dispensers to match above	15.00– 18.00
	#3	Pitcher to match #1,2	20.00– 25.00
Row 2:	#1	Red mug	30.00– 35.00
	#2	Crown Tuscan mug	65.00– 75.00
	#3	Crystal McKee "Bottoms Down" mug	150.00–165.00
	#4	"Elsie" sundae	12.50– 15.00
	#5	Striped cocktail shaker	12.50– 18.00
	#6	Cambridge pinch decanter	55.00– 65.00
Row 3:	#1-7	Comic cocktail shaker set "Sweet Ad-aline"	65.00– 75.00
	#8	Tumbler, 8 oz., matches #9	6.00– 9.00
	#9	Cocktail shaker "Gay 90's" scene	15.00–18.00
	#10	Tumbler, 4 oz., matches #9	10.00–12.00
	#11	New Martinsville "Prelude" cocktail shaker, 32 oz.	85.00–95.00

Page 139

Top:	#1	Seville yellow mixer complete	150.00–200.00
	#2	Top bowl only	20.00– 25.00
	#3	Top bowl juicer insert	75.00–100.00
Bottom:	#1	Chalaine Blue mixer	450.00–500.00
	#2	Top bowl only	50.00– 75.00
	#3	Top bowl juicer insert	250.00–300.00

138

MUGS

More mug collectors are beginning to ask for these items at shows than in the past. You can obtain a small collection without much searching, but after the first twenty or so, you will have to work to find additional ones. Many of these mug collectors are not aware that Kitchenware collectors also seek mugs to go along with their glassware.

The Seville and Jadite "Bottoms Down" mugs on Row 4 always create the most interesting comments from non-collectors. A crystal one is pictured later in the book. At mall antique shows, the little old ladies always look embarrassed about picking one up. Not much later, guess who sneaks back to show a friend?

The most expensive mug is the pink Colonial shown in Row 3. This also comes in green, but only three have ever been found in that color!

The last mug on the bottom row is Moondrops. This mug can be found in several colors as well as two sizes.

Note the ad below for a "Beer Set" featuring the mug shown in Row 3: #3. These sets were made by Hocking and today, would fetch $280.00-315.00 as shown with six mugs. That is up somewhat from the $0.95 price of yesteryear.

Row 1:	#1	Green root beer	30.00– 35.00
	#2	Same pink	25.00– 30.00
	#3	Pink frosted root beer	25.00– 30.00
	#4	Yellow root beer	30.00– 35.00
	#5	Amber	35.00– 40.00
Row 2:	#1	Forest Green, Cambridge	40.00– 45.00
	#2	Yellow, same	35.00– 40.00
	#3	Crystal, Heisey "Old Sand-wich"	20.00– 30.00
	#4	Pink, called "Adam's Rib" by collectors	20.00– 25.00
	#4	Same, green	25.00– 28.00
Row 3:	#1	Colonial, pink, Hocking	450.00–500.00
	#2	Black, "Genolite"	30.00– 35.00
	#3	Green, pretzel, Hocking	30.00– 35.00
	#4	Peacock blue	25.00– 30.00
	#5	Forest Green, Cambridge "Mt. Vernon"	30.00– 35.00
Row 4:	#1	Green soda fountain type	25.00– 28.00
	#2	Same, apple green	25.00– 28.00

Row 4:		(Continued)	
	#3	Seville yellow, McKee "Bottoms Down"	150.00–165.00
	#4	Same, Jadite	150.00–165.00
	#5	Green, Imperial "Chesterfield"	22.00– 25.00
	#6	Same, amber	20.00– 22.50
Row 5:	#1	Red, New Martinsville	22.50– 25.00
	#2	Light blue	22.00– 25.00
	#3	Red, Cambridge "Tally-Ho"	28.00– 30.00
	#4	Green, Hobnail	20.00– 22.00
	#5	Green	20.00– 22.00
	#6	Amber, applied handle	20.00– 22.50
Row 6:	#1	Pink, footed Jeannette	28.00– 32.00
	#2	Same, green	28.00– 32.00
	#3	Green, Fostoria "Priscilla"	15.00– 18.00
	#4	Green	35.00– 40.00
	#5	Cobalt, New Martinsville "Moondrops"	30.00– 35.00

8-PC. BEER SETS
GREEN GLASS . . . OPTIC PATTERN

80 oz. jug, six 12 oz. handled mugs, 10 in. covered pretzel or cookie jar, pressed green glass.
50R-2075—1 set in carton, 12 lbs......Set **.95**

141

NAPKIN HOLDERS

The "Paramount" pink napkin holder shown below sells in the $375.00–425.00 range. This "Paramount" also comes in green and black. You can see a black one on page 137.

The white one shown below says HY-G Napkins on it. It sold for $150.00.

The light blue in Row 2: #3 may be a letter holder; but in any case, it is of foreign manufacture.

Napkin Holders continue to be one of the most difficult kitchenware items to photograph. Most are the same size and shape. Since they are flat, embossed lettering disappears when they are placed in rows. That does not take into consideration the white or black ones. The whites disappear from the photo if you light from the back. The blacks vanish if you light from the front. This is just one of the minor details that we struggle with as we work through our picture taking marathons.

Row 1:	#1	White, NAR-O-FOLD, "Property of trade Nar-O-Fold mark Napkin Company, Chicago, reg. U.S.A.	50.00– 55.00
	#2	Frosted crystal	50.00– 55.00
	#3	Crystal, vertical ribbed	50.00– 55.00
	#4	Black, same as #1	135.00–145.00
Row 2:	#1	Crystal, horizontal ribs, L.E. Smith	50.00– 55.00
	#2	Forest Green	85.00– 95.00
	#3	Light blue, foreign	65.00– 75.00
	#4	White, Paden City "Party Line"	50.00– 55.00
Row 3:	#1	Pink, Paden City "Party Line"	135.00–150.00
	#2	Same, green	125.00–135.00
	#3	Same, black	135.00–145.00

Row 3:		(Continued)	
	#4	Same, crystal	50.00– 55.00
Row 4:	#1	Green "Clambroth," SERV-ALL	175.00–195.00
	#2	Same, opal white	45.00– 55.00
	#3	Same, white	45.00– 55.00
	#4	White, Ft. Howard HANDI-NAP	45.00– 55.00
	#5	White, SLEN-DR-FOLD	50.00– 55.00
Row 5:	#1	White, FAN FOLD, Property of Diana Mfg., Green Bay	75.00– 85.00
	#2	Green, FAN FOLD, no other embossing	120.00–135.00
	#3	Same, Forest green	125.00–135.00
	#4	Green, same as #1	120.00–135.00
	#5	Crystal, same as #2	60.00– 70.00

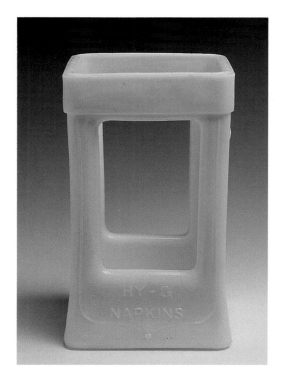

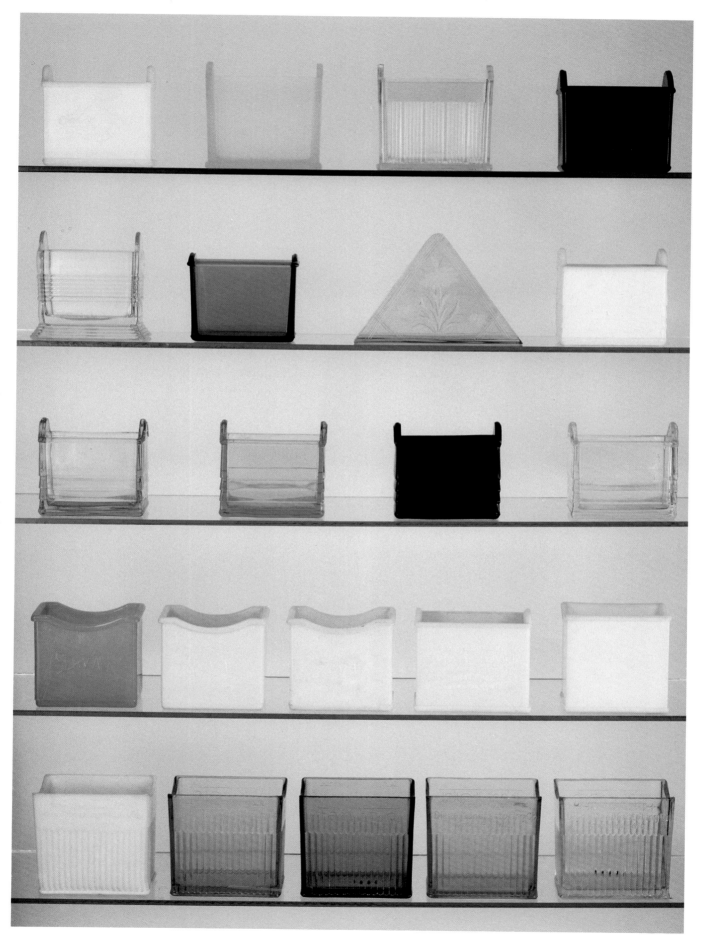

OIL & VINEGAR or FRENCH DRESSING BOTTLES

Fostoria and Cambridge oil and vinegar bottles are in demand by collectors who are looking for the better known etched patterns. While plain or unetched varieties do sell, they do not sell nearly as fast or at as lofty a price. Amber colored bottles are the slowest to sell no matter which company made them or what etching may be on them.

The correct stopper for the pyramid shaped bottle in the bottom row can be seen on page 49. Over the years many bottles had substitute stoppers added. Like lids and cups, many a stopper dropped! Note that colored bottles often have crystal stoppers.

Row 1:	#1	Paden City, green	65.00– 75.00
	#2	Same, pink	65.00– 75.00
	#3	Cambridge, etched pattern, green	85.00– 95.00
	#4	Same, no etching	65.00– 75.00
	#5	Cambridge, amber w/crystal stopper	30.00– 35.00
	#6	Same, w/amber stopper	55.00– 60.00
	#7	Green set (late 1940's)	40.00– 45.00
Row 2:	#1	Cambridge "Rosalie" (#731), pink	100.00–115.00
	#2	Same, green	110.00–125.00
	#3, 5, 7	Cambridge crystal, ea.	22.00– 25.00
	#4	Cambridge w/sterling stopper	50.00– 55.00
	#6	Hawkes, green	85.00– 95.00
Row 3:	#1	Heisey, "Flamingo" pink	75.00– 85.00
	#2	Same, crystal ("Mfg. under license granted by T.G. Hawkes & Co.; Fill w/vinegar to line marked Vinegar, w/oil to line marked Oil, salt & pepper, etc., to taste, shake & you have perfect dressing")	45.00– 50.00
	#3	Heisey "Twist," pink	95.00–105.00
	#4, 9	Fostoria amber, ea.	35.00– 40.00
	#5	Fostoria w/sterling top	22.00– 25.00
	#6, 7	Fostoria, yellow or green	75.00– 80.00
	#8	Fostoria yellow w/crystal top	50.00– 55.00
Row 4:	#1	Paden City "Party Line," pink	55.00– 65.00
	#2	Unknown "pyramid" style (wrong stopper; see p.43)	65.00– 75.00
	#3	Cambridge set, 3 pc. pink	65.00– 75.00
	#4	Crackle set (possibly Cambridge)	40.00– 50.00
	#5	Yellow	25.00– 30.00
	#6	Cambridge pink	25.00– 30.00
	#7	Amber	25.00– 27.50

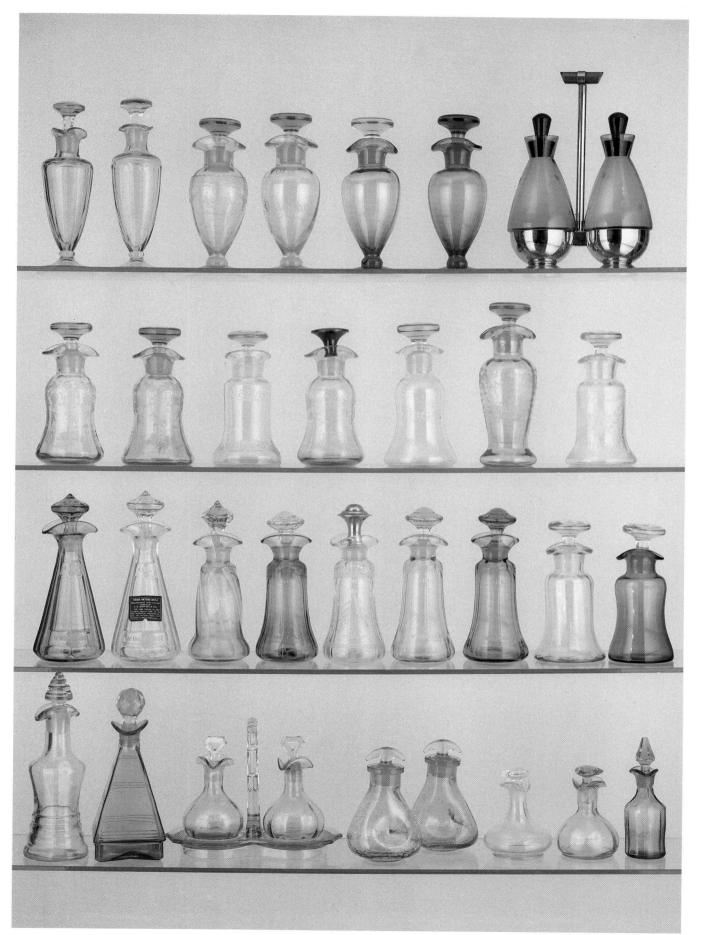

REAMERS, Baby

These two part reamers are twice as difficult to find perfect as the one piece reamers.

The Barnes reamer shown in Row 3 was only the beginning of the repros. Unfortunately, original molds were bought after Westmoreland's demise and used to make some reproductions. The Barnes reamers are all marked with B in a circle. However, Summit Art Glass of Akron, Ohio, is using original molds under a private contract without marking the glass in any way!

Other repros have come from Taiwan. See pages 236 – 237 on reproductions. Items with an asterisk below have been reproduced. To keep abreast of all the reamer news I suggest you join the national reamer club. The address is as follows: National Reamer Collectors Association, c/o Larry Brandstad, 405 Benson Rd. W., Frederic, WI 54837-8945.

Westmoreland Glass Company (Rows 1-3)

Row 1:	#1	Pink, 2 piece	150.00–175.00
	#2	Same, crystal	45.00– 55.00
	#3	Blue (bottom only $90.00-100.00)	200.00–225.00
	#4	Amber, 2 piece	175.00–200.00
	#5	Sun-colored-amethyst (bottom only $40.00-45.00)	80.00– 90.00
	#6	Green, 2 piece	175.00–200.00
Row 2 & 3:		**Bottom is worth ⅔ of price except where noted below.**	
*Row 2:	#1	Frosted pink	110.00–125.00
	#2	Green (top & bottom about equal in value)	200.00–225.00
	#3	Crystal w/decorations	35.00– 40.00
	#4	Pink (bottom value $20.00-25.00)	125.00–150.00
	#5	Frosted blue bottom only	40.00– 45.00
	#6	Sun-colored-amethyst (SCA)	50.00– 60.00
*Row 3:	#1	Frosted crystal (decorated add $10.00)	45.00– 50.00
	#2	Pink decorated	125.00–140.00
	#3	Blue (bottom value $25.00-30.00)	155.00–175.00
	#4, 5	NEW! RUBINA AND COBALT BLUE MARKED WITH B IN CIRCLE INSIDE CONE OF TOP AND ON BOTTOM OF BASE	
		SEE PAGE 235 FOR ADDITIONAL COLORS.	
Row 4:	#1	L.E. Smith (top rare), pink	250.00–275.00
	#2	Same, green	250.00–275.00
	#3	Same, crystal (in metal add $5.00)	20.00– 30.00
	#4	Jenkins, green	125.00–150.00
	#5	Same, crystal	30.00– 35.00
	#6	Same, frosted crystal	40.00– 45.00
Row 5:	#1	Unknown, blue (top $200.00)	450.00–450.00
	#2	Unknown, pink (top $100.00)	175.00–200.00
	#3	Unknown, crystal (top $10.00)	15.00– 20.00
	#4	Unknown, frosted crystal "Baby's Orange"	50.00– 65.00
	#5	Unknown, crystal	25.00– 35.00
	#6	Unknown, frosted crystal decorated "Baby"	85.00– 95.00
Row 6:	#1	Unknown, crystal	35.00– 40.00
	#2	Unknown, crystal, called "Button & Bows"	45.00– 60.00
	#3	Unknown, crystal probably foreign (emb. sword & hammer)	30.00– 35.00
	#4	Unknown, crystal, "thumbprint" design	45.00– 50.00
	#5	Unknown, crystal, notched top	45.00– 50.00
	#6	Unknown, crystal	30.00– 40.00
Row 7:	#1	Unknown, decorated crystal, "Orange Juice"	55.00– 60.00
	#2	Unknown, frosted decorated crystal	85.00–100.00
	#3	Unknown, pink (possibly foreign)	125.00–150.00
	#4	Fenton, SCA (sun-colored-amethyst) (bottom $55.00)	70.00– 80.00
	#5	Fenton, elephant decorated base	65.00– 75.00

REAMERS, Fenton, Fry, Foreign, Federal and Indiana

The following three pages show the vast price ranges reamer collectors face. Reamers come in all shapes, sizes, and colors. The names in quotes with the Fry reamers are the company names for each color.

The foreign reamers on page 150 represent a separate collecting field in themselves. Not enough information is known about this vast field of reamers. There are many unique shapes and colors to attract a collector to these reamers made outside the United States.

Page 149

Row 1:	#1	Fenton pitcher & reamer set, red	1,000.00–1,200.00
		(top is ⅓ price; bottom is ⅔ on these)	
	#2	Same, black	1,200.00–1,400.00
	#3	Same, blue	2,000.00–2,500.00
	#4	Same, jade	850.00– 950.00
Row 2:	#1	Same, transparent green, top only	200.00– 225.00
	#2	Fry, straight side, "Azure" blue	1,500.00–1,750.00
	#3	Same, light green	22.50– 25.00
	#4	Same, "Emerald" green	30.00– 35.00
Row 3:	#1	Same, "Pearl" opalescent white	25.00– 30.00

Row 3:		(Continued)	
		Same, embossed "Blue Goose"	200.00–250.00
	#2	Same, "Canary" vaseline	45.00– 50.00
	#3	Same, "Rose" pink	45.00– 55.00
Row 4:	#1	Same, crystal	18.00– 20.00
	#2	Same, "Amber"	300.00–325.00
	#3	Same, "China" white	600.00–800.00
Row 5:	#1	Fry, fluted reamer (jello mold) "Canary"	300.00–325.00
	#2	Same, "Emerald" green	450.00–500.00
	#3	Same, "Rose"	175.00–200.00
Row 6:	#1	Same, "Pearl"	40.00– 40.00
	#2, 3	Tufglas, light or dark	85.00– 95.00

Foreign Reamers
Page 150

Row 1:	#1	Pinkish amber	40.00– 45.00
	#2, 5	Cobalt blue or amber	100.00–110.00
	#3	Smoke	75.00– 85.00
	#4	Yellowish custard	90.00–100.00
Row 2:	#1, 5	Pink or light pinkish amber	40.00– 50.00
	#2, 3	Embossed "Foreign," 2 piece, green or pink	40.00– 50.00
	#4	Yellow	125.00–140.00
Row 3:	#1, 3, 5	Root Beer, blue & light yellow, ea.	100.00–110.00
	#2	Embossed "Tcheco-Scovaquie" on handle, crystal	40.00– 50.00
	#4	Embossed sword & hammer on handle	15.00– 20.00
Row 4:	#1, 5	Crystal, last has "K" inside shield mark, ea.	15.00– 20.00
	#2	Light yellow top only	65.00– 75.00
	#3, 4	Pink or "Coke" bottle green	45.00– 55.00

Row 5:	#1, 2, 4 & 5	Light green, amber, amethyst or pinkish amber, ea.	60.00– 70.00
	#3	Crystal	25.00– 30.00
Row 6:	#1	Light turquoise	50.00– 55.00
	#2	Green, marked "Argentina"	125.00–150.00
	#3, 5	Cornflower blue or light green	100.00–125.00
	#4	Crystal, embossed fruit	50.00– 60.00
Row 7:	#1, 2	Crystal Czechoslovakia or pink	40.00– 50.00
	#3, 4	Light turquoise or diamond shaped crystal (Rb No 517385)	35.00– 40.00
	#5	Pink	90.00–110.00
	#6	Amber	110.00–125.00

Page 151
Rows 1-3 Federal Glass Company

Row 1:	#1	Ribbed, loop handle, pink	30.00– 35.00
	#2	Same, amber	17.50– 20.00
	#3	Panelled, loop handle, green	25.00– 30.00
Row 2:	#1	Same, amber	20.00– 25.00
	#2	Tab handle, yellowish/-amber	275.00–300.00
	#3	Same, green	22.00– 25.00
	#4	Tab handled, ribbed, seed dam, green	22.00– 25.00
Row 3:	#1	Same, pink	90.00–100.00
	#2, 3	Tab handled amber, ea.	15.00– 20.00
	#4	Green, pointed cone	22.00– 25.00

Row 4:	#1	Amber, handled, spout opposite	250.00–300.00
	#2	Same, crystal	22.00– 25.00
	#3	Same, pink	75.00– 85.00
Row 5:	#1	Same, green	32.00– 35.00
	#2	Crystal, horizontal handle	18.00– 20.00
	#3	Same, green	20.00– 25.00
Row 6:	#1	Crystal, emb. ASCO, "Good Morning, Orange Juice"	20.00– 25.00
	#2	Amber, six sided cone, vertical handle	250.00–300.00
	#3	Same, green	65.00– 75.00
	#4	Same, pink	125.00–150.00

Rows 4-6 **Indiana Glass Company**

REAMERS, Hazel Atlas and Hocking Glass Companies

The Hazel Atlas 2-cup reamer pitcher has been the plague of novice collectors and dealers for several years. This has been newly made in cobalt blue, pink, and an odd green color. **See Reproduction Section on pages 236 – 237 for items with asterisk.**

Page 153 All Hazel Atlas Glass Company

Row 1:	#1	Yellow 2 cup pitcher and reamer set	325.00–350.00
	#2	Same, cobalt blue	*275.00–295.00
	#3	Same, pink	*125.00–145.00
	#4	Same, green	*35.00– 40.00
Row 2:	#1	Crisscross, cobalt blue	275.00–295.00
	#2	Same, pink	250.00–295.00
	#3	Same, crystal	15.00– 18.00
	#4	Same, green	25.00– 30.00
Row 3:	#1	Green, tab handled	22.00– 25.00
	#2, 3	Decorated 2 cup sets, ea.	35.00– 38.00
	#4	Fired-on red set	40.00– 45.00
Row 4:	#1, 3-5	Decorated sets, ea.	35.00– 38.00
	#2	Tumbler to match #1	10.00– 12.00
Row 5:	#1	Crisscross, tab handled, pink	300.00–325.00
	#2	Same, green	25.00– 30.00
	#3	Same, crystal	15.00– 18.00
	#4	Green, tab handled	22.00– 25.00

Page 154 All Hazel Atlas Glass Company

Row 1:	#1	Reamer pit., 4 cup marked A&J, green	35.00– 40.00
	#2	Same, A & J, Pat Applied For, crystal	20.00– 25.00
	#3	Green, 4 cup, ftd.	30.00– 35.00
	#4	Green, stippled pitcher	30.00– 35.00
Row 2:	#1, 2	Tab handle, lemon, pink, light or dark	35.00– 40.00
	#3	Same, green	22.00– 25.00
	#4	Same, white w/red trim	22.50– 25.00
Row 3:	#1-3	White, w/decorated trim, 4 cup	30.00– 35.00
	#4	White, 4 cup, stippled pitcher	30.00– 35.00
Row 4:	#1	Small tab handled reamer, pink	35.00– 40.00
	#2	Same, green	22.00– 25.00
	#3	Same, cobalt blue	300.00–325.00
	#4	Large tab handled reamer, pink	35.00– 40.00
Row 5:	#1	Same, white	35.00– 40.00
	#2	Same, cobalt blue	275.00–295.00
	#3	Same, crystal	10.00– 12.00
	#4	Same, green	22.00– 25.00

Page 155 All Hocking or Anchor Hocking Glass Company

Row 1:	#1	"Circle" pitcher w/reamer top	65.00– 70.00
	#2	Pitcher reamer, 4 cup, ftd., green	30.00– 35.00
	#3	Pitcher reamer, 4 cup, flat, green	30.00– 35.00
Row 2:	#1	Pitcher reamer, 2 cup, green	35.00– 40.00
	#2	Same, Vitrock	30.00– 35.00
	#3	Pitcher reamer, ribbed, 2 cup	60.00– 65.00
	#4	Same, crystal	22.50– 25.00
Row 3:	#1	Pitcher reamer, 4 cup, crystal	30.00– 32.00
	#2	Vitrock, tab	85.00–100.00
	#3	Green "Clambroth," tab	150.00–175.00
	#4	Pitcher top, "Mayfair blue"	300.00–350.00
Row 4:	#1-3	Orange reamer, loop handle, green, ea.	20.00– 25.00
Row 5:	#1	Same, Vitrock	20.00– 25.00
	#2	Fired-on black tab	12.50– 15.00
	#3	Green tab	22.00– 25.00

154

REAMERS, Fleur-de-Lis, Jeannette, and Miscellaneous

The reamers shown on Page 157 are found mainly on the West coast. I am astonished at the diversity of tints of opaque red found on Fleur-de-Lis reamers. A fleur-de-lis emblem is embossed on the side of most of these. (If not, it is listed as unembossed.) The opalescent red shades are quite stunning particularly when they are exhibited in an illuminated cabinet.

Price differences are controlled by color variations, whether there are emblems or not or whether the reamers possess rims or not.

Note the large Delphite reamer Row 3, #4 on Page 159. There have been few of these found!

Page 157

Row 1:	#1	"VALENCIA," white (embossed word)	90.00–100.00
	#2	Same, crystal	150.00–200.00
	#3	Same, green	175.00–200.00
Row 2:	#1	Plain, no embossing, "VALENCIA"	75.00– 85.00
	#2	Same, opalescent white	50.00– 60.00
	#3	Same, pink	150.00–200.00
	#4	Same, pinkish amber	250.00–300.00
Row 3:	#1, 4	"Fleur-de-Lis," red/orange slag	350.00–425.00
	#2	Same, amberina/opalescent	550.00–650.00
	#3	Same, mustard/slag	375.00–450.00

Row 4:	#1	Embossed white "Fleur-de-Lis"	75.00– 85.00
	#2	Same, red/orange slag	350.00–425.00
	#3	Same, red	425.00–500.00
	#4	Same, root beer	550.00–600.00
Row 5:	#1	Same, crystal	175.00–200.00
	#2	Unembossed, grayish custard	125.00–150.00
	#3	Same, custard w/"rim edge"	135.00–150.00
	#4	Same, white w/"rim edge"	40.00– 60.00
Row 6:	#1	"LINDSAY," pink	375.00–425.00
	#2	"LINDSEY," pink	375.00–425.00
	#3	"LINDSAY," green	400.00–450.00

Page 158

Row 1:	#1	Large crystal (called "monster")	35.00– 40.00
	#2	Light turquoise, O J extractor	100.00–125.00
	#3	Foreign, pink	65.00– 75.00
	#4	Crystal, Glasbake, McKee on handle	50.00– 75.00
Row 2:	#1	Hazel Atlas old reamer (recently iridized)	75.00– 95.00
	#2	Green "log" handle	100.00–125.00
	#3	Crystal	12.50– 15.00
	#4	"Colony" like, twin spout	*15.00– 20.00
		Same, white	150.00–200.00
	#5	Foreign, amber	80.00– 85.00
Row 3:	#1	"Clambroth," "British make," embossed	175.00–200.00
	#2	"MacBeth-Evans Glass Co., Charleroi, Pa."	200.00–250.00
	#3	"Clambroth," boat shaped	150.00–200.00
Row 4:	#1	Black, "Orange Juice Extractor"	350.00–400.00

Row 4:	(Continued)		
	#2	Same, green	45.00– 50.00
	#3	Same, pink	100.00–125.00
	#4	Same, "Clambroth"	75.00– 8500
Row 5:	#1	Green, like #2, but unembossed	150.00–200.00
	#2	Crystal, embossed "Sunkist Oranges & Lemons" or "Los Angeles Fruit Growers Exchange," ea.	25.00– 35.00
	#3	Pink, unembossed	185.00–200.00
Row 6:	#1	Crystal, square, marked Italy	12.50– 15.00
	#2	"Easley's," (called "chisel cone")	65.00– 75.00
	#3	"Easley's," square opalescent white	150.00–200.00
	#4	"Read," some embossed, some not	100.00–125.00
	#5	Unusual six sided top	45.00– 50.00

Page 159 All Jeannette Glass Company

Row 1:	#1	"Hex Optic" bucket reamer, pink	40.00–	45.00
	#2	Same, green	40.00–	45.00
	#3	2 cup reamer pitcher	110.00–	120.00
	#4	Delphite, w/top (see page 24)	1,250.00–	1,500.00
Row 2:	#1	Crystal, large, loop handle	12.00–	15.00
	#2	Same, green	22.00–	25.00
	#3	2 cup reamer pitcher, light Jadite	30.00–	35.00
	#4	Same, dark Jadite matching top/bottom	75.00–	85.00
Row 3:	#1	Small, Delphite	85.00–	95.00
	#2	Large, dark Jadite	30.00–	35.00

Row 3:	(Continued)			
	#3	Same, light Jadite	25.00–	30.00
	#4	Same, Delphite	1,000.00–	1,250.00
Row 4:	#1	Small, dark Jadite	30.00–	32.00
	#2	Same, light Jadite	28.00–	30.00
	#3	"Jennyware," crystal	100.00–	110.00
	#4	Same, pink	110.00–	125.00
	#5	Same, ultra-marine	110.00–	125.00
Row 5:	#1	Green, 5" tab reamer	20.00–	25.00
	#2	Green, 5$^{7}/_{8}$" tab reamer	20.00–	25.00
	#3	Same as #1, crystal	8.00–	10.00
	#4	Same as #2, pink	35.00–	40.00
	#5	Same as #1, pink	35.00–	40.00

REAMERS, Cambridge and McKee

McKee Glass Company made most of the Sunkist reamers, though not all. **According to records just uncovered at the Fenton factory, the very first Sunkist reamers were made by Indiana Glass Company.**

The McKee symbol is an "McK" with a circle around it and said insignia adds interest to a reamer. Collectors of reamers concern themselves with color, type (lemon, orange, grapefruit), handles, spouts, seed dams or not, footed or flat bottomed, embossing, size and shape of the reaming section, etc. As usual, scarcity and demand determine price for reamers, many of which are not cheap!

Page 161

Row 1:	#1	Cambridge green	175.00– 200.00	Row 3:		(Continued)	
	#2, 3	Same, light pink	175.00– 200.00			Same, pink, (not shown)	750.00– 400.00
Row 2:	#1	Same, amber	600.00– 700.00			Same, cobalt blue, (not shown)	900.00– 1,000.00
	#2	Same, green w/silver Rockwell decoration	250.00– 300.00		#4	Grapefruit, ultra-marine	750.00– 850.00
	#3	Cambridge, crystal	20.00– 25.00	Row 4:	#1	Same, Seville yellow	210.00– 225.00
		Same, Cobalt blue (shown page 21)	2,000.00–2,500.00		#2	Same, flat yellow	225.00– 250.00
					#3	Same, custard	600.00– 650.00
Row 3:	#1	Cambridge, small tab, crystal	12.50– 15.00	Row 5:	#1	Same, "Caramel"	750.00– 850.00
	#2	Same, cobalt blue	300.00– 350.00		#2	Same, black	1,100.00– 1,200.00
	#3	Cambridge, small, ftd., green	450.00– 500.00		#3	Same, white	250.00– 350.00
		Same, crystal, (not shown)	20.00– 22.00	Row 6:	#1	Same, Jadite	150.00– 175.00
					#2	Same, Chalaine blue	750.00– 850.00
					#3	Same, pink	750.00– 850.00

Page 162 All embossed "SUNKIST" unless noted.

Row 1:	#1	Green opalescent "fry"	200.00–225.00	Row 4:		(Continued)	
	#2	Opalescent "fry"	110.00–125.00		#2	Jadite	30.00– 35.00
	#3	Transparent ultra-marine	800.00–850.00		#3	Dark Jadite, slightly opalescent	175.00–195.00
	#4	Butterscotch "fry"	800.00–850.00		#4	Olive green milk glass	750.00–850.00
Row 2:	#1	Lilac pinkish white	85.00– 95.00	Row 5:	#1	Transparent green	45.00– 50.00
	#2	Pink	50.00– 60.00		#2	Unembossed green	200.00–250.00
	#3	Light pink	50.00– 60.00		#3	Forest Green	700.00–750.00
	#4	Pinkish amber	200.00–225.00		#4	Vaseline green	40.00– 50.00
Row 3:	#1	"Blocked" letters in "SUNKIST," swirl	300.00–350.00	Row 6:	#1	Seville yellow	40.00– 55.00
	#2	Black	700.00–750.00		#2	Yellowish custard	30.00– 35.00
	#3	Chalaine blue	200.00–225.00		#3	Custard	30.00– 35.00
	#4	Chocolate	700.00–750.00		#4	Greenish custard	75.00– 85.00
Row 4:	#1	Turquoise blue milk glass	400.00–450.00				

Page 163 "SUNKIST" Rows 1-3

Row 1:	#1	Ivory	125.00–150.00	Row 4:		(Continued)	
	#2	Gray	150.00–175.00		#2	Same, Custard	45.00– 50.00
	#3	Opal white (value determined by opalescence)	50.00–145.00		#3	Jadite, unembossed, smaller foot than embossed below in Row 6	30.00– 35.00
	#4	White	7.00– 10.00	Row 5:	#1	White, "McK" embossed	18.00– 20.00
Row 2:	#1	"Blocked" letters in "SUNKIST," white	100.00–120.00		#2	Same, Custard	18.00– 20.00
	#2	Opal Crown Tuscan	350.00–385.00		#3	Same, Jadite	30.00– 35.00
	#3	Crown Tuscan milk glass	350.00–385.00		#4	Same, Delphite	275.00–325.00
	#4	Caramel variation	350.00–385.00	Row 6:	#1	White, 6", "McK" embossed	30.00– 35.00
Row 3:	#1	Caramel, light	350.00–385.00		#2	Same, Custard w/red trim	25.00– 30.00
	#2	Caramel, medium	350.00–385.00		#3	Same, Jadite	30.00– 35.00
	#3	Caramel, butterscotch	350.00–385.00		#4	Same, Delphite	600.00–650.00
	#4	Mustard	350.00–385.00				
Row 4:	#1	Skokie Green, pointed cone, 5¼"	55.00– 60.00				

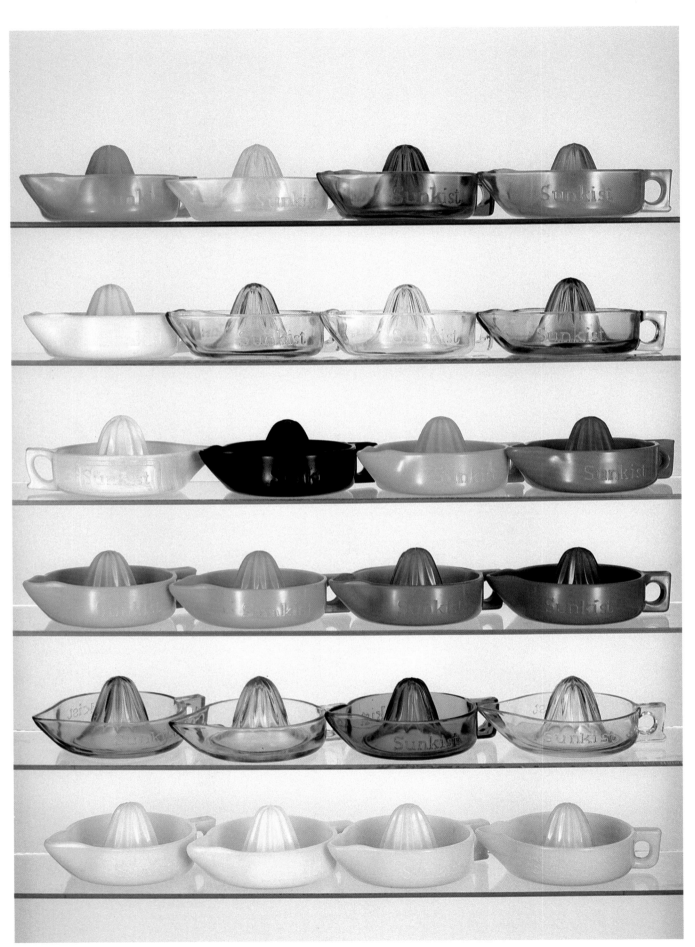

REAMERS, Paden City, Westmoreland, and U.S. Glass Companies

You can find numerous cocktail shaker bottoms missing their metal reamer tops. That metal top is a hard to find item, so don't buy too many topless cocktail shakers expecting to find a top. To my knowledge, there are no replacements for these available. See **Reproduction Section pages 236 – 237** for items with asterisks.

There are *several different* inserts for the U.S. Glass reamers. The pitcher in Row 1, #1 and the tubs in Row 2 on Page 166 each have a $4^{1}/_{2}$" diameter reamer top. A $4^{1}/_{8}$" top fits the other pitchers on Page 166 *and* the slick handled, horizontal ribbed two cup pitchers on that page. That $4^{1}/_{8}$" top fits all the loop handled two cup pitchers on Page 167, but the insert for the four cup pitchers is $5^{1}/_{8}$" in diameter.

Page 165

Row 1:	#1	Pink cocktail shaker/ reamer, "Party Line"	60.00– 65.00
	#2	Same, amber	100.00–110.00
	#3	Green, cocktail shaker/ reamer, "Speakeasy"	40.00– 45.00
	#4	Pink pitcher & reamer top	200.00–250.00
		Same, crystal pitcher w/black handle & top (shown page 171)	300.00–350.00
	#5	Green, 4 cup pitcher & top, "Party Line"	125.00–135.00
Row 2:	#1	Same, pink	125.00–135.00
	#2	Same, crystal complete	60.00– 65.00
		Same, turquoise blue complete	350.00–400.00
		Same, black (shown page 171)	500.00–550.00

Row 2:	(Continued)		
	#3	Westmoreland, green, 2 piece, embossed orange/lemon	*150.00–175.00
	#4	Same, pink	*150.00–175.00
Row 3:	#1	Same, crystal	*175.00–195.00
	#2, 3	Westmoreland, crystal decorated oranges or lemons, flattened loop handle, ea	*55.00– 65.00
Row 4:	#1	Same, dark green	*90.00–110.00
	#2	Same, light green	*90.00–110.00
	#3	Same, bluish green	*125.00–140.00
Row 5:	#1	Same, white	*200.00–250.00
	#2	Same, pink	*85.00– 95.00
	#3	Same, amber	*200.00–250.00

Page 166 All U.S. Glass Company

Row 1:	#1, 4	Reamer pitcher set, 3 piece, pink, ea.	250.00–275.00
	#2	Reamer pitcher set, green	250.00–275.00
		Same, yellow, shown on page 87	650.00–750.00
	#3	Tumbler for set	10.00– 12.50
Row 2:	#1	Tub, w/reamer top, pink	150.00–200.00
	#2	Same, green	150.00–200.00
	#3	"Vidrio Products No. J-50"	150.00–165.00
	#4	Slick handle, 2 piece, horizontal ribs, (each rib is $1/_2$ cup) amber	300.00–325.00
Row 3:	#1	Slick handle, green, insert near top of cup (graduated measurements on side)	35.00– 40.00

Row 3:	(Continued)		
	#2	Same, pink	35.00– 40.00
	#3	Same as Row 2, #4, pink	35.00– 40.00
	#4	Same, frosted pink	25.00– 30.00
Row 4:	#1	Same, green	35.00– 40.00
	#2	Same, turquoise blue	85.00–100.00
	#3	Same, crystal	22.50– 25.00
	#4	Same, frosted green	30.00– 35.00
Row 5:	#1	Slick handle, barred or vertical ribs	60.00– 65.00
	#2	"Handy Andy," green (note reamer cone differs)	40.00– 50.00
	#3	Crystal, same as #1	22.00– 25.00

Page 167 All U.S. Glass Company

Row 1:	#1	4 cup pitcher set, amber	500.00–550.00
	#2	Same, green	125.00–145.00
	#3	Same, pink	275.00–295.00
Row 2:	#1	2 cup, pitcher set, light pink	40.00– 45.00
	#2	Same, dark pink	40.00– 45.00
	#3	Same, white	125.00–150.00
	#4	Same, amber	300.00–325.00
Row 3:	#1	Same, yellow (light honey amber)	300.00–325.00
	#2	Same, blue complete	600.00–750.00
		Same, crystal, complete	20.00– 25.00
	#3, 5	Same, crystal, decorated, ea.	20.00– 25.00

Row 3:	(Continued)		
	#4	Tumbler, matching reamer	7.50– 10.00
Row 4:	#1	Same, frosted green	25.00– 30.00
	#2	Same, bluish green (turquoise)	100.00–115.00
	#3	Same, dark green	40.00– 45.00
	#4	Same, light green	40.00– 45.00
Row 5:	#1	Slick handle, light pink	120.00–135.00
	#2	Same, dark pink	120.00–135.00
	#3	Same, amber	300.00–325.00
Row 6:	#1	Same, white	75.00– 85.00
	#2	Same, green	90.00–100.00
	#3	Slick handle, grapefruit	400.00–450.00

REAMERS, Miscellaneous, Mechanical and Unusual

This remains the "catch-all" section on reamers. Reamers not fitting previous categories go here. Many of the glass reamer manufactures are unknown, although I am sure that McKee made the Saunders and most likely the Radnt. However, to my knowledge, no valid catalogue information has ever surfaced to prove that.

I shall repeat the RE-GO reamer story as shown in Rows 3 and 5 on page 169. I find it unbelievable that these ever survived being used. It is a mechanical, glass, two part reamer. The only thing separating the glass from crunching together is a small wooden peg that allows the insert to be turned by hand to extract the juice.

The name RE-GO comes from a reamer that originally said "puRE-GOld." (The small letters in pure gold were placed there for emphasis by me.) The PURE-GOLD reamer itself may never have been marketed; the first name was altered by removing the letters "p, u, l, d" to leave the name RE-GO. The old letters can still be seen on these reamers, albeit slightly.

The green insert shown in Row 3 #1 is called "EASY SQUEEZE" and is used on a similar base as that of the RE-GO.

The crystal pitcher on Page 171 in Row 2, #3 has to have a **black handle** and **black top** for price listed.

Page 169

Row 1:	#1	Jadite, embossed SAUNDERS	1,250.00–1,450.00
	#2	"Sanitary Bess Mixer," (embossed **"4"** inside a large **"1"**)	175.00– 200.00
	#3	"Ideal" Pat'd Jan 31, 1888	125.00– 175.00
	#4	Black, same as #1	1,250.00–1,400.00
Row 2:	#1	"Tricia," black	1,400.00–1,500.00
	#2	Same, pink complete	700.00– 800.00
		Same, crystal complete	350.00– 400.00
	#3	Same, green	700.00– 800.00
Row 3:	#1	"EASY SQUEEZE," green top only	200.00– 250.00
		Same, complete (not shown)	500.00– 550.00
	#2	Green RE-GO	400.00– 500.00
	#3	RE-GO crystal top only	125.00– 150.00
		Same, complete (not shown)	300.00– 400.00
Row 4:	#1	"RADNT," crystal	95.00– 115.00
	#2	Same, green	350.00– 450.00
	#3	Same, pink	350.00– 450.00
Row 5:	#1	RE-GO, opalescent white	550.00– 650.00
	#2	Same, blue	1000.00–1,250.00
	#3	Same, black (top shown)	1000.00–1,250.00

Page 170

Row 1:	#1	Metal insert	125.00–145.00
	#2	Glass insert, probably Hocking	250.00–275.00
	#3	Mount Joy	200.00–225.00
Row 2:	#1	"Mayfair" blue glass insert, probably Hocking	550.00–600.00
	#2	"SUNKIST JUNIOR" mechanical reamer, "clambroth"	100.00–125.00

Page 171

Row 1:	#1	Hocking "Mayfair" blue 2 cup reamer pitcher	1,400.00–1,500.00
Row 2:	#1	Paden City "Party Line," black	500.00– 550.00
	#2	Morgantown, green	200.00– 250.00
	#3	Morgantown, crystal pitcher, black handle & top	300.00– 350.00

ROLLING PINS

Rolling pin reproductions have caused my mail box to fill up for about two years. A word of warning to those of you who may have found a colored rolling pin with a screw-on metal lid. No "old" rolling pins with screw-on metal lids have ever been found in any transparent color other than crystal. If you have pink, cobalt blue, red, or an odd shade of green, then you have a "recent vintage" rolling pin!

The abundance of crystal rolling pins has not noticeably diminished. These sell in the $10.00–12.00 range. Dealers who sell primitives or crafts are filling these with marbles, beans, and other colorful things to sell them. I saw one around Easter with jelly beans priced at $25.00!

Shown below are some new additions to the listing: black and "Robin Egg" blue. Both of these are the blown type shown on page 175.

Page 172

Row 1:	#1 Black	400.00–450.00
	#2 "Robin Egg" blue	400.00–450.00

Page 173 McKee Glass Company except for last row

Row 1: Note circular band opposite shaker top end.
#1	Jadite	400.00–450.00
#2	Custard	325.00–350.00

Row 2 & 3: Note smooth end opposite shaker top end on these rows.

	#1	Seville yellow	325.00– 350.00
	#2	Delphite blue	1,500.00–1,800.00
Row 3:	#1	Chalaine blue	1,500.00–1,800.00
	#2	Jadite	400.00– 450.00
Row 4:	#1	Crystal w/screw-on cobalt handles	225.00– 250.00

Wooden Handles
Page 174

Row 1:		Peacock blue (handles attached to metal rod inside pin)	250.00–275.00
Row 2:	#1	Green transparent (handles attached to wood dowel pin)	450.00–500.00
	#2	Pink (screw-on wooden handles)	450.00–500.00
Row 3:	#1	White (comes w/wood or metal screw-on handles), ea. marked "Imperial Mfg. Co., Cambridge, Ohio"	75.00– 85.00
		Same, Custard color (not shown)	140.00–165.00
	#2	Cobalt blue (handles attached to metal rod inside pin)	400.00–450.00
Row 4:		Clambroth white (screw-on wood handles)	100.00–125.00

Blown Rolling Pins
Page 175

Row 1:	#1	Amethyst	120.00–135.00	Row 3:	#1	Peacock blue, dark	175.00–200.00
	#2	Cobalt blue	150.00–200.00		#2	Crystal, "Kardov Flour, Famous Self Rising"	50.00– 60.00
Row 2:	#1	Amber, light	100.00–120.00	Row 4:	#1	Chalaine blue	400.00–450.00
	#2	Forest green	125.00–150.00		#2	Blue, light	175.00–225.00

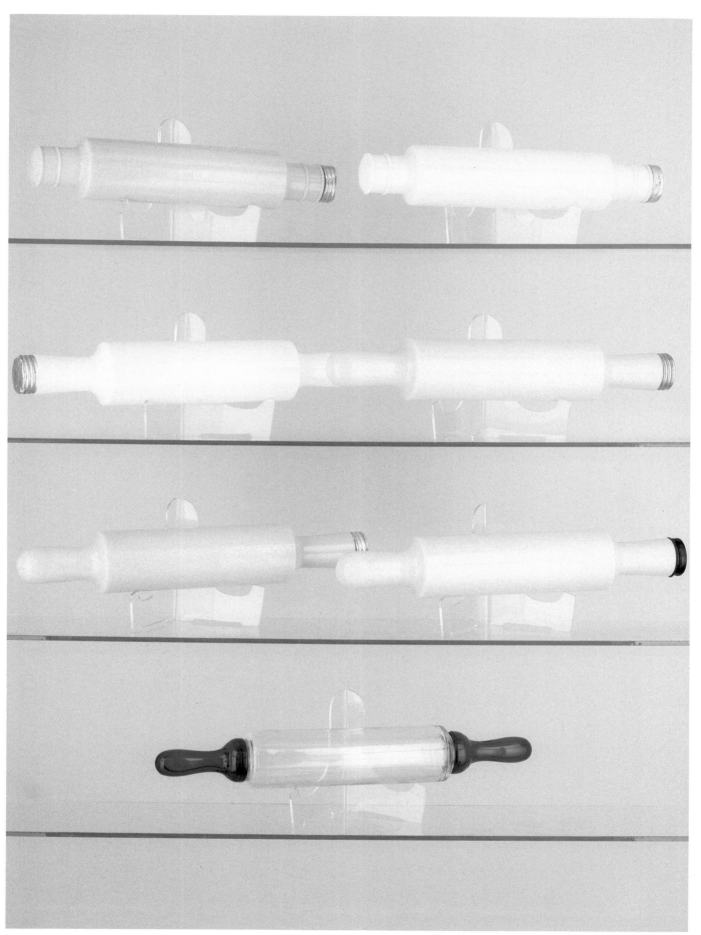

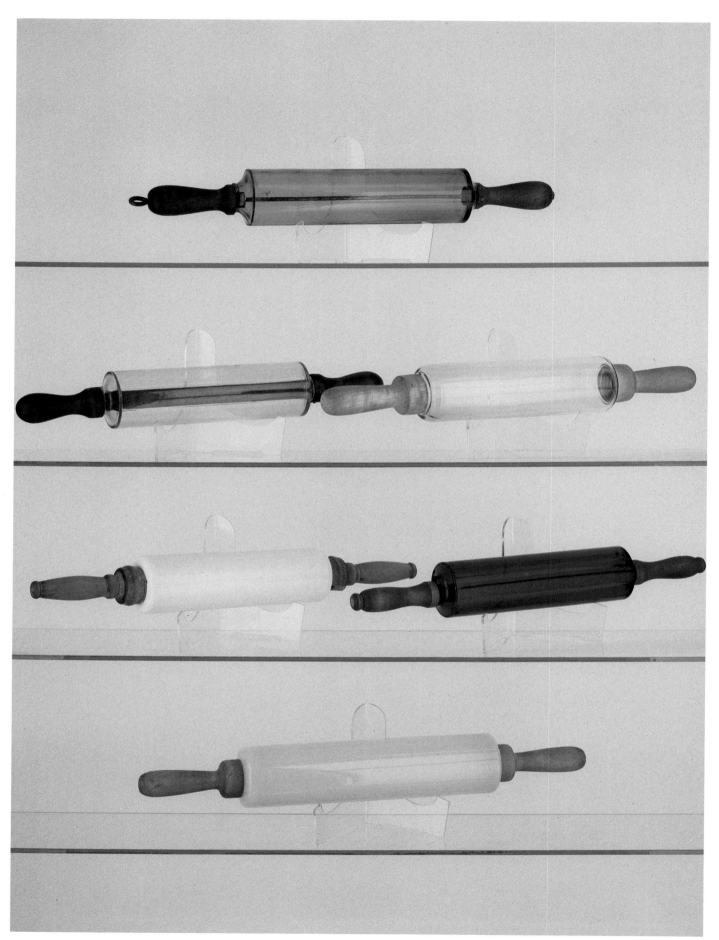

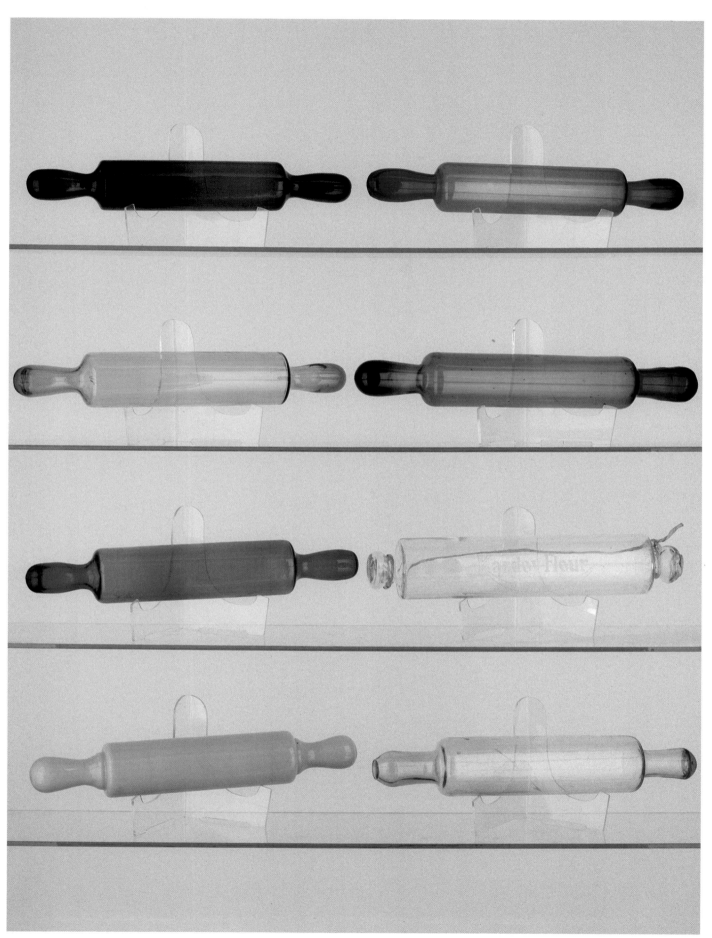

SALAD SETS and ADDITIONAL LADLES

Prices of the colored sets have soared, especially those from the Cambridge, Imperial, or Heisey companies. Items made by major glass companies of that time are always more collectable than unidentified glassware.

The inclusion of salad sets in the Kitchen book opened a new collecting field for some buyers who were not aware of the variety available before then. Many of these sets were of foreign manufacture — mainly Czechoslovakia.

Forks and spoons sell for around the same price, but there seems to be a small premium ($1.00–5.00) for a set. A few remaining ladles that would not fit in that section are included on page 179.

Prices below are for sets unless otherwise noted. (Take half of the lowest price listed for one piece only.)

Page 177

Row 1:
#1	Blue, large pointed handle set		50.00–60.00
#2	Amber set		30.00–40.00
#3	Yellow, small pointed handle set		30.00–40.00
	Same, pink (not shown) marked "TCHECOBLOV"		40.00–50.00
#4, 5	Green set		40.00–50.00
#6-9	Same, peacock or cobalt blue set		55.00–70.00
#10	Same, red set		75.00–85.00
#11, 12	Boxed forks, green or pink, ea		25.00–30.00

Row 2:
#1, 2	Long crystal handled amber set		30.00–35.00
#3, 4	Red teardrop handle set		50.00–60.00
	Same, cobalt blue (not shown)		45.00–55.00
	Same, amethyst (not shown)		40.00–50.00
#5	Green top and bottom set		40.00–50.00
#6	Blue spoon		27.50–35.00
#7, 8	Green set		50.00–60.00
#9	Amber flattened stripped handle set		30.00–40.00

Row 3:
#1, 2	Forest green set		40.00–45.00
#3, 4	Black handled set		55.00–65.00
#5, 6	All amber set, found with Czechoslovakia labels		40.00–50.00
#7	White set, serrated and waffle back		40.00–50.00
#8	Canary yellow or vaseline, set		70.00–80.00

Page 178

Row 1:
#1, 2	Cobalt blue, rounded, ribbed handle set		50.00–55.00
#3, 4	Same, green		40.00–45.00
#5, 6	Same, light blue		50.00–55.00
#7, 8	Same, amber		25.00–35.00
#9	Same, crystal		20.00–22.50
	Same, pink (not shown)		40.00–45.00

Row 2:
#1	Blue w/crystal top, set		45.00–50.00
#2, 3	Forest green flattened handle set		45.00–55.00
#4, 5	Pink set, edge down sides		45.00–50.00
#6, 7	Same, cobalt blue		50.00–55.00
#8, 9	Same, amber		30.00–35.00

Row 3:
#1	Blue pointed fork, set		45.00–55.00
#2, 3	Amber flattened handle set		30.00–35.00
#4	Same, pink		45.00–50.00
#5, 6	Same, green		45.00–50.00
#7, 8	Amber set		35.00–40.00
#9-11	Amber 3 piece set		65.00–75.00
	Same, cake server only		35.00–40.00

Page 179

Row 1: **All Cambridge Glass Company**
#1, 2	Crystal set w/label		40.00– 45.00
#3-6	Black or light blue		125.00–150.00
#7, 8	Amber		65.00– 75.00
#9	Green set		100.00–110.00
#10	Red set		175.00–200.00
	Same, cobalt blue (not shown)		200.00–250.00

Row 2:
#1, 2	Light blue set, **Imperial** (box shown $5.00)		75.00– 85.00
#3, 4	Same, amber		55.00– 65.00
#5, 6	Same, green		75.00– 85.00
#7, 8	Pink set, possibly Imperial		75.00– 85.00
#9, 10	Same, blue		100.00–110.00

Row 3: **Ladles**
#1	Green		35.00– 45.00
#2	Same, crystal		30.00– 35.00
#3	White, black handle/measure on side of ladle		45.00– 50.00
#4	Crystal, large		12.00– 15.00

178

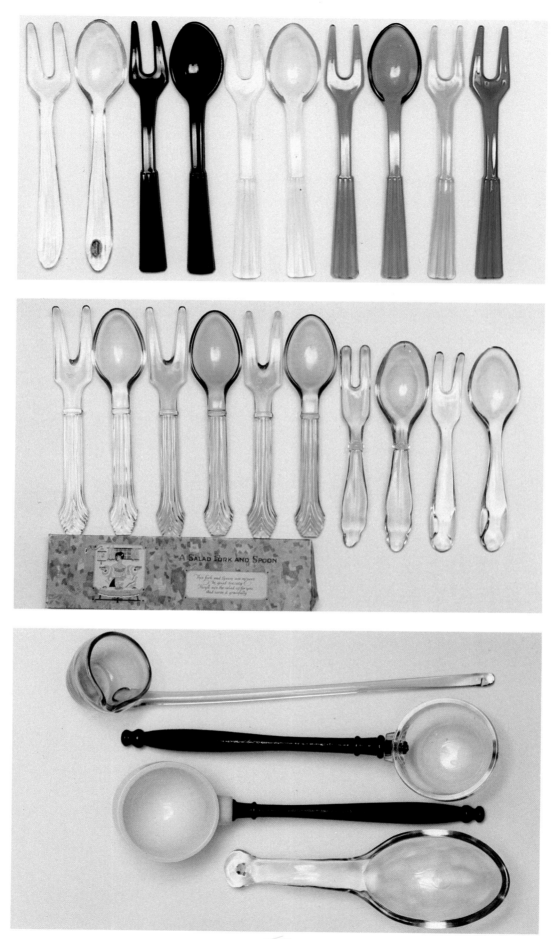

SALT BOXES

Salt boxes are another of the items that few collectors buy per se, but many are bought by collectors of color or by collectors buying sets. The "Zipper" or the "Sneath" canister sets are not complete without the salts shown here. There is considerable demand for these latter types and they sell very quickly on the market.

Crystal salt boxes are gathered by collectors looking to complete "Hoosier" or comparable kitchen cabinet spice and canister sets. I have seen some very high prices on these in shops that sell "primitive" antiques. What I wonder is, "Do they actually sell for those prices?"

Row 1:	#1	Crystal w/glass lid, embossed SALT, Flintext	90.00–100.00
	#2	Jadite, Mckee	75.00– 85.00
	#3	Same, Chalaine blue	175.00–200.00
Row 2:	#1	Green "Zipper" w/lid	150.00–175.00
		Same, wo/lid	100.00–125.00
	#2	Peacock blue	125.00–150.00
	#3	Green "Sneath"	225.00–250.00
Row 3:	#1	Jadite w/lid, Jeannette	250.00–275.00
	#2	White, embossed SALT box	100.00–125.00
	#3	White, round embossed SALT box	100.00–110.00
Row 4:	#1	Crystal, "Sneath"	15.00– 20.00
	#2	Amber "Sneath"	125.00–150.00
	#3	Crystal, embossed SALT	12.00– 15.00
	#4	Crystal, "Zipper"	10.00– 12.00
Row 5:	#1	Green Jeannette round embossed SALT on lid	200.00–225.00
	#2	Crystal salt w/lid	15.00– 17.50
	#3	Crystal, ribbed, embossed SALT	10.00– 12.50
	#4	Crystal, ribbed	8.00– 12.00

SHAKERS, Hocking, Hazel Atlas, Owens Illinois, Tipp City

Please note that the previously listed "kitchen cabinet shakers" shown on page 185 Row 4, #5, 6 were strictly vacuum cleaner attachments used for blowing moth crystals into your closet. Two readers have definitely confirmed this with vacuum advertising! Live and learn!

See Reproduction Section pages 236 – 237 for items marked with asterisk.

Page 183

Row 1:	#1-5	Shakers, ea.	5.00– 6.00
	#6	Shaker or spice set in rotating tray	25.00–30.00
	#7	Tall yellow shaker	8.00–10.00
	#8	Amber shaker	10.00–12.50
	#9,10	Hocking opaque yellow, ea.	15.00–18.00
Row 2:	#1-16	Cattail, shakers ea.	3.00– 4.00
Row 3:	#1,2	Delphite "basket wave" pr.	25.00–30.00
	#3	Delphite blue "Roman Arch" pepper	75.00–80.00
	#4	Sellers spice shaker	10.00–12.00
	#5	Hocking, crystal	3.00– 4.00
	#6	Owens-Illinois green	7.50– 8.00
	#7	Green, plain	6.00– 7.00
	#8	Green, "Moisture Proof"	50.00–55.00
	#9,10	Jennyware, flat, pink, pr. w/labels	65.00–70.00

Row 3:	(Continued)		
	#11	Amber	12.50–15.00
Row 4:	#1,2	Hazel Atlas "Skating Dutch" flour or sugar	12.50–15.00
	#3,4	Hocking "Modern Tulips" salt or pepper	7.50–9.00
	#5-7	Roastmeat seasoning	30.00–35.00
		Same, salt or pepper	10.00–12.00
	#8,9	"Clambroth" white embossed salt or pepper	20.00–22.50
Row 5:	#1	Black pepper	15.00–20.00
	#2	Black sugar	20.00–25.00
	#3-6	Scotty dog salt or pepper	10.00–12.50
		Flour or sugar	15.00–17.50
	#7	Sitting bird pr.	15.00–20.00
	#8,9	Black flour or sugar	20.00–25.00

Hocking Glass Company (Rows 1-3)
Page 184

Row 1:	#1-4	Opaque yellow, ea.	15.00–18.00
	#5-7	Fired-on yellow, ea.	4.00– 6.00
	#8-10	Fired-on blue, ea.	10.00–12.00
Row 2:	#1	Fired-on green	7.00– 9.00
	#2, 3	Panelled fired-on blue, ea.	8.00–10.00
	#4-6	Green Clambroth, panelled, ea.	17.50–20.00
	#7, 8	Transparent green, ea.	15.00–18.00
	#9, 10	Vitrock, ea.	8.00–10.00
Row 3:	#1	Crystal w/raised dots	4.00– 5.00
	#2	Clambroth	8.00–10.00
	#3	Green, plain	9.00–11.00
	#4	Tulip (lid is valued at $1.00-2.00)	6.00– 8.00
	#5, 7 & 8	White, ea.	6.00– 8.00
	#6	Green Jad-ite	8.00–10.00
	#9	Green, round	20.00–25.00
Row 4:	#1, 2	Hazel Atlas embossed pink salt or pepper	*40.00–45.00
	#3	Same, crystal	20.00–25.00

Row 4:	(Continued)		
	#4, 5	Same, green salt or pepper	*30.00–35.00
	#6, 7	Same, flour or sugar	75.00–85.00
	#8	Dutch salt	12.50–15.00
	#9, 10	White w/green, ea.	10.00–12.00
Row 5:	#1-4	White w/black, ea.	10.00–12.00
	#5, 6	Black fired-on, ea.	8.00–10.00
	#7	Owens-Illinois ovoid shape (good lettering)	15.00–17.50
	#8, 9	Same, square shapes	8.50–10.00
	#10, 11	Sneath, amber, ea.	20.00–27.50
Row 6:	#1	Crystal, embossed celery	4.00– 5.00
	#2, 3	Crystal, embossed salt & sugar, ea.	5.00– 6.00
	#4	Green, embossed flour	35.00–40.00
	#5	Green	30.00–40.00
	#6	"Clambroth"	12.00–15.00
	#7	"Clambroth"	10.00–12.50
	#8	Black, round	17.50–20.00
	#9	Black	17.50–20.00
	#10	Black, ribbed	18.00–20.00

Page 185

Row 1:	#1, 2	Lady salt or pepper	20.00–22.50
	#3, 4	Same, flour or sugar	22.50–25.00
	#5, 6	Jadite, ea.	17.50–20.00
	#7, 8	"Art Deco," pr.	40.00–45.00
	#9, 10	Blue, pr.	18.00–22.00
	#11, 12	Fired-on blue, pr.	10.00–12.00
Row 2:	#1	Fired-on Dutch set	25.00–30.00
	#2	Dutch white set	15.00–17.50
	#3	Lady watering set (goes with Row 2 on previous page)	30.00–36.00
Row 3:	#1	Singing birds set	25.00–30.00

Row 3:	(Continued)		
	#2, 3	Scotty dogs, ea.	7.50– 9.00
	#4	Rooster set	10.00–12.50
	#5, 6	"Sombrero Sam" set	25.00–30.00
	#7, 8	White set w/salt dehumidifier	12.50–15.00
Row 4:	#1, 2	Black set (w/good lettering)	35.00–40.00
	#3, 4	Uncle Sam's hat set	10.00–12.50
	#5, 6	Vacuum cleaner attachments for blowing moth crystals, ea.	12.00–15.00
	#6-9	Floral or cherry, pr.	10.00–12.00

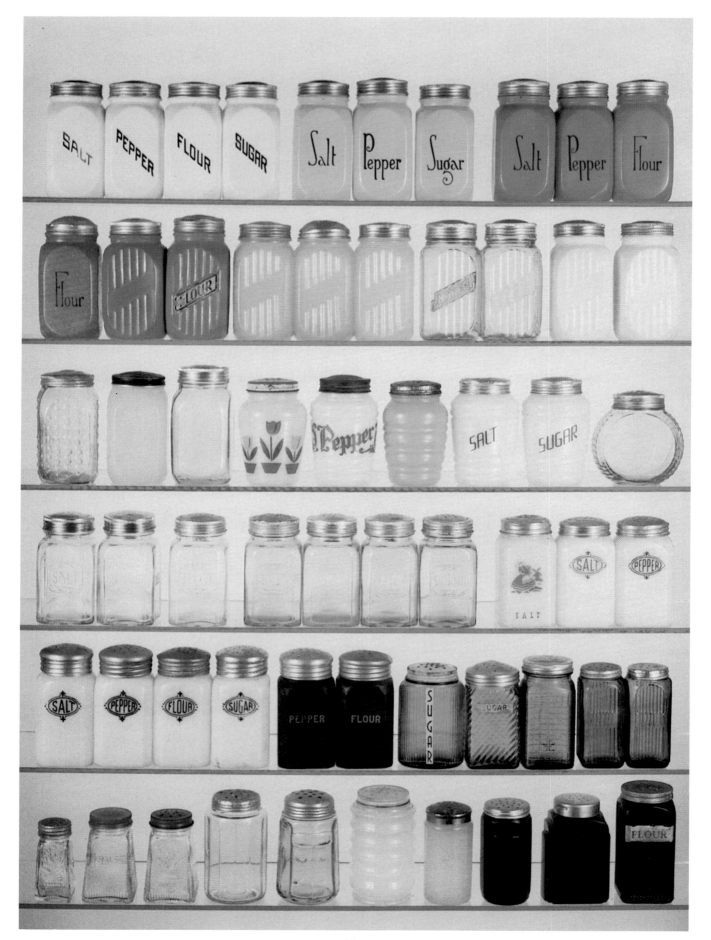

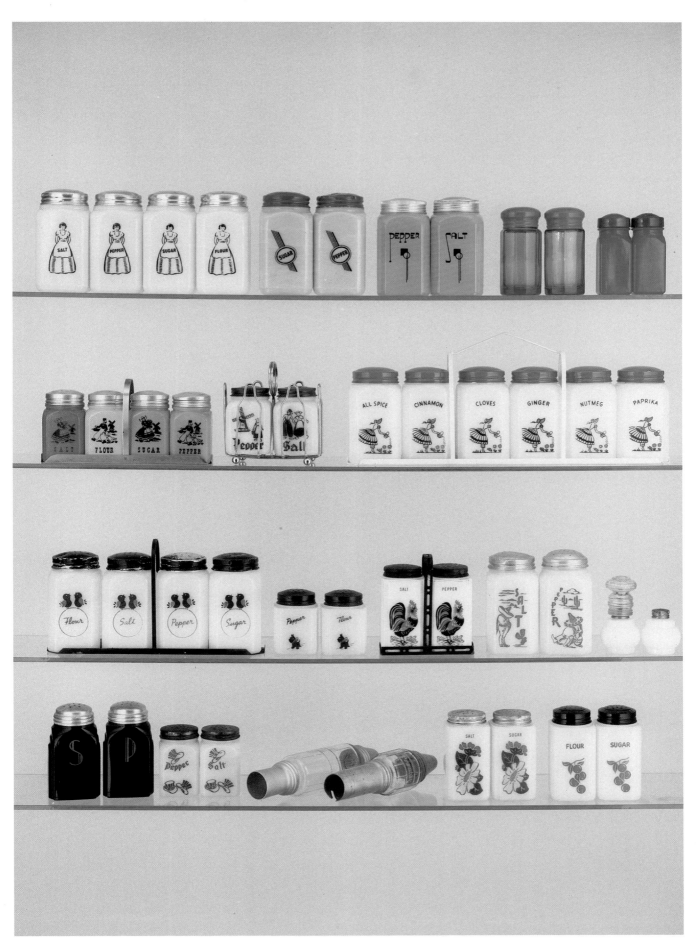

SHAKERS, Jeannette, McKee, etc.

All blue shakers are in demand, but there has also been an increase in demand for white and the later issued Fire King sets. New collectors start with the inexpensive sets and graduate to higher priced sets. Generally speaking, it would be better to buy the more expensive sets first! That is, if you can find them to buy!

Availability of all shakers has decreased in recent years. There are more salt and peppers found than other shakers, but one major problem with these heavily used items is worn lettering. Mint lettering on salt shakers is a premium! There were fewer flour, sugar, and spice sets made than salt and pepper sets. Possibly extra shakers came with grease sets and likely, ladies just did not buy shakers for flour and sugar!

Jeannette Glass Company (first 4½ rows)
Page 187

Row 1:	#1, 2	Delphite blue, 8 oz., salt	45.00– 50.00
		pepper	40.00– 45.00
	#3	Same, sugar	100.00–120.00
	#4	Same, paprika	100.00–115.00
	#5, 6	Jadite, decorated salt/pepper, ea.	12.00– 15.00
	#7, 8	Same, mouth wash or bicarbonate soda	90.00–110.00
	#9, 10	Jadite, 6 oz. w/o label, ea.	6.00– 8.00
Row 2:	#1,2	Jadite light, salt or pepper	10.00– 12.00
	#3,4	Same, flour or sugar	12.00– 15.00
	#5	Jadite dark, pepper	9.00– 11.00
	#6	Same, flour	11.00– 13.00
	#7, 8	Delphite blue, square, salt or pepper	75.00– 85.00
	#9	Same, flour or sugar	85.00– 95.00
Row 3:	#1, 2	Jadite dark, square, salt or pepper	15.00– 17.50
	#3, 4	Same, flour or sugar	20.00– 22.50
	#5, 6	Jadite light, square, salt or pepper	15.00– 17.50

Row 3:	(Continued)		
	#7, 8	Same, flour or sugar	20.00–22.50
	#9	"Jennyware" pink	18.00–20.00
Row 4:	#1-4	"Jennyware" ultra-marine (subtract $1.00 missing label), ea.	22.00–25.00
	#5-8	Same, crystal	6.00– 8.00
Row 5:	#1-4	"Jennyware" flat shaker, pink, ea.	27.50–30.00
	#5	Same, crystal	18.00–20.00
	#6	Green, sold as sugar shaker	35.00–40.00
	#7	Unknown manufacturer, green "Zipper"	35.00–40.00
	#8	Crystal, "Zipper"	18.00–20.00
Row 6:	#1	Green, embossed flour	40.00–50.00
	#2	Crystal, embossed salt	18.00–20.00
	#3	Crystal, embossed allspice	18.00–20.00
	#4	Crystal, embossed cinnamon	18.00–20.00
	#5	Crystal, ribbed	10.00–12.00
	#6-11	Sneath green, ea.	40.00–50.00

McKee "Roman Arch" Shakers
Page 188

Row 1:	#1	Skokie green, salt	22.50–25.00
	#2-4	Same, pepper, flour or sugar	20.00–25.00
	#5	Same, cinnamon	35.00–38.00
	#6, 7	Delphite blue, salt or pepper	75.00–80.00
	#8-10	Fired-on colors, ea.	8.00–10.00
Row 2:	#1-9	"Dots," salt or pepper	15.00–17.50
	#1-9	Same, flour or sugar	22.50–25.00
	#10	Custard w/green flour	12.00–15.00
Row 3:	#1,2	Custard salt or pepper	10.00–12.00
	#3,4	Same, flour or sugar	12.00–15.00
	#5, 6	"Diamond Check," pr. on white	30.00–35.00
	#7, 8	"Dots" on white, pr.	20.00–24.00

Row 3:	(Continued)		
	#9, 10	Fired-on red, pr.	16.00–20.00
Row 4:	#1,2	White w/black, salt or pepper, ea.	12.00–15.00
	#3,4	Same, flour or sugar, ea.	20.00–22.00
	#5-7	White w/red, ea.	9.00–11.00
	#8, 9	Crystal, frosted, ea.	6.00– 7.00
Row 5:	#1-11	Black, pepper ($15.00-20.00) all others w/good lettering	20.00–25.00
		Black w/o lettering	6.00– 8.00
Row 6:	#1-4	Fired-on colored set	16.00–20.00
	#5	"Bow," red on white	10.00–12.00
	#6, 7	"Ships," salt or pepper	9.00–10.00
	#8, 9	Same, flour or sugar	10.00–12.00

McKee "Square" Shakers
Page 189

Row 1:	#1-3	Large, 16 oz., ea.	40.00– 45.00
	#4-7	Small, 8 oz., ea.	10.00– 12.00
	#8, 9	Skokie green, pr.	25.00– 30.00
Row 2:	#1, 2	Embossed dark jade salt or pepper	45.00– 50.00
	#3, 4	Same, flour or sugar	50.00– 55.00
	#5	Embossed Chalaine blue, ea.	125.00–150.00
	#6-9	Chalaine blue, ea.	90.00– 95.00
Row 3:	#1	White, salt, ea.	10.00– 12.00
	#2, 3	Flour or sugar, ea.	18.00– 20.00
	#4-8	"HOTPOINT" or "ELECTROCHEF" embossed white, ea.	8.00– 10.00
	#9, 10	White, ea.	9.00– 10.00
Row 4:	#1, 2, 5, 6	Skokie, green salt or pepper	15.00– 17.50
	#3, 4, 7	Same, flour or sugar	20.00– 22.50

Row 4:	(Continued)		
	#8	Same, "Cinnamon"	25.00–30.00
	#9, 10	Black w/o good lettering ($8.00-10.00) w/lettering, ea.	15.00–20.00
Row 5:	#1, 2	Custard, ea. salt or pepper	10.00–12.00
	#3, 4	Flour or sugar	17.50–20.00
	#5, 6	Same, ginger, cinnamon, nutmeg w/good lettering, ea.	25.00–30.00
	#8	Seville yellow, salt or pepper	12.00–15.00
	#9, 10	Same, flour or sugar	16.00–18.00
Row 6:	#1, 2	Seville yellow, salt or pepper	12.00–15.00
	#3, 4	Same, flour or sugar	16.00–18.00
	#5, 6	Skokie green, dark, salt or pepper, ea.	15.00–17.50
	#7, 8	Same, flour or sugar, ea.	20.00–22.50

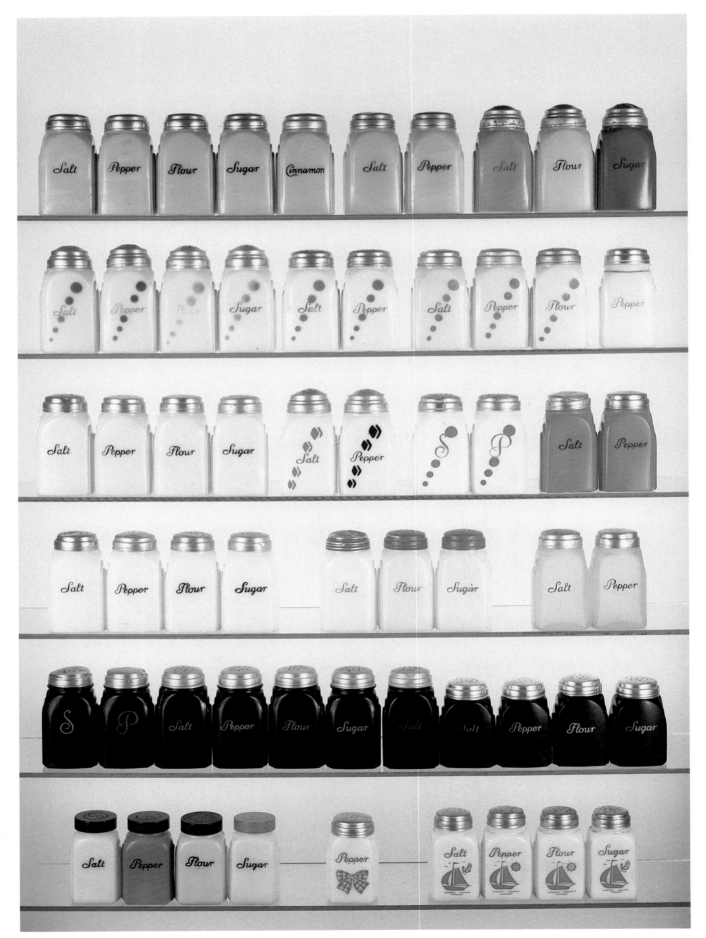

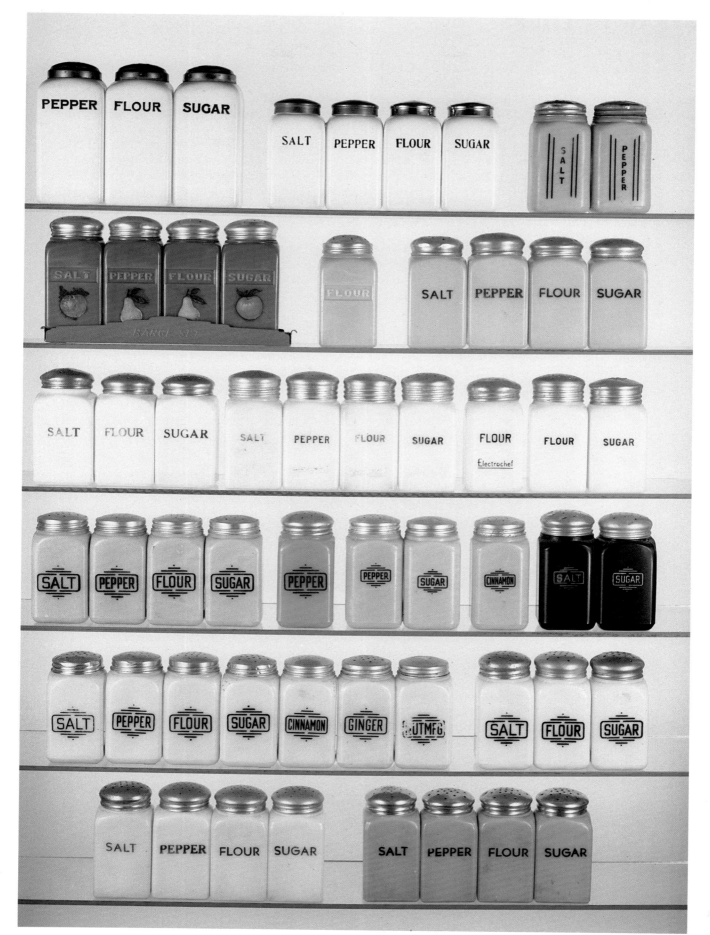

STRAW HOLDERS

Unfortunately, the biggest news on straw holders regards reproductions. Beware of any odd colored jars with a diamond design around the base. This design is similar to that on page 193, row 1, #2. These are being made in pink, an odd shade of green, and cobalt blue at the present. By the time you read this there may be additional colors. When you see a new metal insert — **beware** — it could be a newly made jar! As with any purchase, either know from whom you are buying, or if the price seems **too good to be true**, it usually is.

Collectors are still buying that Imperial pink vase to use as a straw jar. There has never been an **old** pink straw jar found. The straw jars shown on page 191 are out of a collection that I was able to borrow for this photograph. The pink straw jar (Imperial vase) shown in the last row is the same one pictured on page 192. Straw jars are among the items that can be found at antique advertising shows. Many collectors, today, have one of these "soda fountain" remembrances. We have one in our kitchen that had a lot of use when our kids were younger. They wouldn't drink a beverage without a straw!

Page 191

Row 1:	#1	Black	600.00–700.00
	#2	Green, tall	400.00–450.00
	#3	Green, short w/fancy metal base	450.00–500.00
	#4,5	Green, short, ea.	350.00–400.00
Row 2:	#1-4	Green, short, ea.	350.00–400.00
		(Some dealers ask a premium for jointed straw lifters)	
	#5	Pink, Imperial vase (used as straw jar, but is vase)	75.00–100.00

Page 192

Row 1:	#1	Cobalt blue, 12" (vase or straw jar?)	200.00–250.00
	#2, 3	Crystal Heisey w/top	225.00–275.00
	#4	Crystal Heisey "Greek Key" w/o lid (metal lid	125.00–150.00
		belongs page 193, Row 1, #2) w/glass lid	275.00–300.00
	#5	Pink, Imperial vase (used as straw jar, but is vase)	75.00–100.00
Row 2:	#1	Crystal, w/metal base	175.00–200.00
	#2	Crystal	75.00– 90.00
	#3	Green, short	350.00–400.00
	#4	Green, short w/fancy metal	450.00–500.00
	#5	Crystal, tall	110.00–150.00

Page 193

Row 1:	#1	Crystal, "Pattern Glass," zipper design, w/lid	225.00– 275.00
	#2	Crystal, w/metal base and lid (lid put on Greek	
		Key jar on page 180 by mistake)	125.00– 150.00
	#3	Emerald Green "Coca Cola"	1,000.00–1,200.00
	#4	Crystal knobbed lid (Candlewick collectors notice	
		this first)	150.00– 200.00
	#5	Crystal, "Pattern Glass," w/lid	250.00– 275.00
Row 2:	#1	Red, later made, possibly late 1950's/early 1960's	150.00– 200.00
	#2	Crystal, jointed straw lifter	100.00– 125.00
	#3	Crystal, named "Manhattan"	150.00– 200.00
	#4	Crystal, cut design on jar	100.00– 125.00
	#5	Crystal, zippered design, missing lid	75.00– 100.00
	#6	Amber, "English Hobnail," vase or straw jar	75.00– 85.00

191

SUGAR SHAKERS

The bullet shaped sugar shakers with indented dots near the top have been found with McKee papers.

Page 195

Row 1:
#1, 2	Cambridge, #732, pink (ewer cream $35.00–40.00)	115.00–125.00
#3, 4	Cambridge #732, green (tall ewer cream $35.00–40.00)	110.00–125.00
#5	Cambridge, blue	150.00–160.00
#6, 7	Cambridge, amber (syrup w/cover $45.00–50.00)	75.00– 85.00

Row 2:
#1, 2	Cambridge, pink (ewer cream $25.00–30.00)	85.00– 95.00
#3	Cambridge, amber, crystal foot & glass top	75.00– 90.00
#4, 5	Same, pink (ewer cream $25.00–30.00)	100.00–110.00
#6, 7	Heisey "Yeoman," pink (cream $25.00–30.00); (add $10.00–15.00 w/glass top)	75.00– 80.00
#8	Cobalt blue	225.00–250.00
#9	Green, w/green screw-in top	200.00–225.00

Row 3:
#1, 2	Green or pink, footed ("Tilt-a-spoon")	275.00–295.00
#3, 4	Green, 2 shades, possibly Paden City	165.00–195.00
#5	Same, cobalt blue	900.00–950.00

Row 3: (Continued)
#6	Same, amber	250.00–275.00
#7	Paden City, pinched in, amber	225.00–250.00
#8	Same, green	200.00–225.00

Row 4:
#1	Green, Hocking	150.00–175.00
#2	Green, Hocking	150.00–175.00
#3	Unknown	95.00–125.00
#4	Green, "Hex Optic"	175.00–195.00
#5	Amber	95.00–125.00
#6	Unknown, pink	125.00–150.00
#7	Pink, w/red top	175.00–200.00
#8	Paden City "Party Line," pink	100.00–125.00

Row 5:
#1	Crystal, Paden City, 2 part dispenser	15.00– 18.00
#2	Crystal, L.E. Smith	35.00– 40.00
#3	Crystal, "West Sanitary Automatic Sugar"	20.00– 25.00
#4, 5	Crystal, Hazel Atlas & unknown, ea.	12.50– 15.00
#6	Crystal, faintly marked "Czechoslovakia"	20.00– 25.00

Page 196

Row 1:
#1	Lancaster Glass Co., "Beehive," green	175.00–200.00
#2-7	"Bullet" shape made by both Jeannette & Paden City	
#2, 3	Green	175.00–200.00
#4	Yellow	275.00–300.00
#5	Pink	200.00–250.00
#6	Crystal	25.00– 35.00
#7	Pink	200.00–250.00

Row 2:
#1	Blue, "Monroe Mfg. Co., Elgin, Ill., Pat Pend." (liquid)	200.00–250.00
#2	Same, pink	150.00–175.00
#3, 4	Green or pink, footed	200.00–250.00
#5	Green	200.00–225.00

Row 3:
#1	Jeannette, light jade	60.00– 70.00
#2-4	Same, pink decorated, green or yellowish jade, ea.	65.00– 75.00
#5-7	Jeannette, pink or green	60.00– 85.00
#6	Same, frosted pink	50.00– 65.00
#8	Green, cone top	85.00– 95.00

Row 4:
#1	White "Clambroth"	40.00– 45.00
#2, 3	Green or pink	40.00– 45.00
#4, 5	Orange or forest green	125.00–150.00
#6	Red	150.00–175.00
#7	Amber, horseshoe pattern	35.00– 40.00
#8	Green, older style	35.00– 45.00
#9	Crystal, marked sugar & cinnamon	18.00– 20.00

Page 197

Row 1:
#1	Yellow fired-on w/red top	18.00– 20.00
#2	Crystal, McKee, indented dots at top	30.00– 40.00
#3	Ultra-marine, Jeannette	250.00–275.00
#4	Same, green	175.00–195.00
#5	Cobalt blue	175.00–200.00
#6	Crystal, cone top	30.00– 35.00
#7	Fired-on red	18.00– 20.00

Row 2:
#1	Amber	200.00–250.00
#2	Pink	200.00–250.00
#3	Black	325.00–375.00
#4	Green	175.00–200.00
#5	SCA (sun colored amethyst)	65.00– 75.00
#6, 7	Hex Optic green or pink	175.00–195.00

Row 3:
#1, 2	Heisey, pink or green	125.00–150.00
#3	Same, crystal	50.00– 55.00
#4	Green	155.00–175.00
#5	Pink, measured teaspoon	175.00–200.00
#6	Blue, marked "Made in Japan" (New!)	5.00– 10.00
#7, 8	Pink or green	80.00–100.00

Row 4:
| #1 | Green | 175.00–200.00 |

Row 4: (Continued)
#2	Pink, Paden City "Rena" Line 154	200.00–250.00
#3	Same, crystal	30.00– 35.00
#4	Same, green	175.00–200.00
#5	Amber	150.00–200.00
#6	Blue	200.00–250.00
#7	Amber	200.00–225.00

Row 5:
#1	Pink, Jeannette	75.00– 85.00
#2	Same, dark Jadite	65.00– 75.00
#3	Green	95.00–110.00
#4	Forest green, Owens Illinois	18.00– 20.00
#5	Green, individual sugar	95.00–110.00
#6	Same, amber	95.00–110.00
#7	Green, handled	100.00–125.00

Row 6:
#1	Crystal, decorated flowers	12.50– 15.00
#2	Crystal "Rena" Line, Paden City	22.00– 25.00
#3	Crystal, zippered design	20.00– 25.00
#4, 8	Crystal, ea.	25.00– 30.00
#5	Crystal, Fostoria "American"	60.00– 65.00
#7	Crystal, "Beehive"	40.00– 45.00

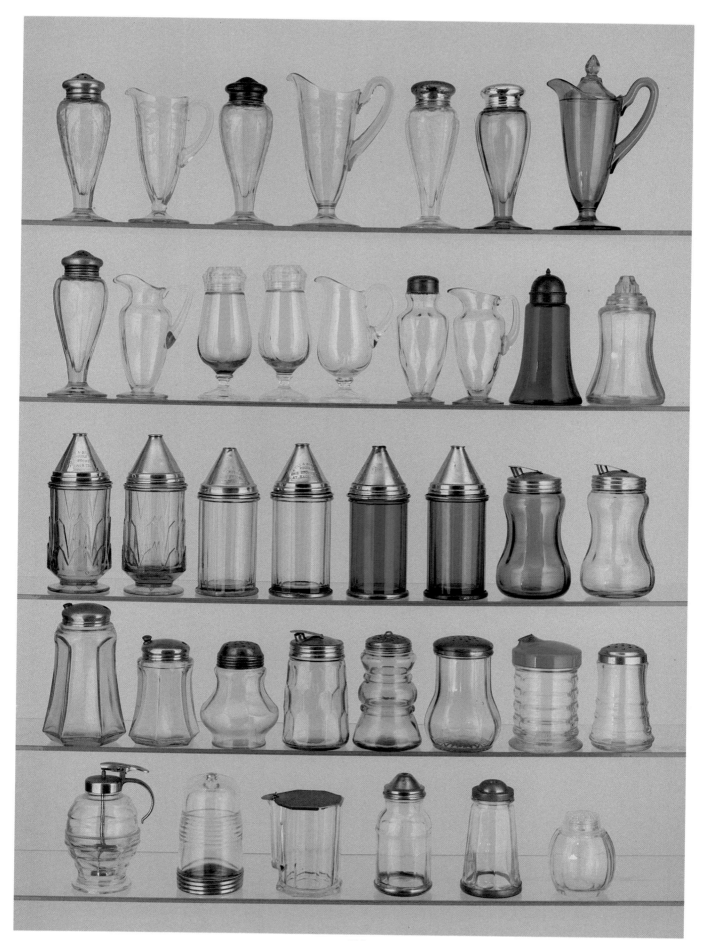

SYRUP PITCHERS

As with many of the other item collections, it is the major glass companies' syrup pitchers that are noticed first.

The number of people I've encountered in my travels who collect syrup pitchers is phenomenal even to me. Somewhere during the conversation, they generally speak of attractive displays, fascinating shapes or colors. Generally, they carry pictures!

Row 1:	#1	Cambridge, w/cover, amber	50.00– 65.00
	#2	Same, green	65.00– 75.00
	#3	Paden City, green	40.00– 45.00
	#4	Imperial, w/slotted lid, pink	70.00– 75.00
	#5	Same, amber	65.00– 70.00
Row 2:	#1	Hazel Atlas, pink	60.00– 65.00
	#2	Same, green	40.00– 45.00
	#3	Same, pink	60.00– 65.00
	#4	Hazel Atlas, pink	60.00– 65.00
	#5	Hazel Atlas, green	50.00– 55.00
	#6	Same, pink	60.00– 65.00
Row 3:	#1, 2	Fostoria "Mayfair," green or pink w/underliner	55.00– 65.00
	#3	Fostoria "Chintz"	200.00–250.00
	#4	Fostoria, "Mayfair," yellow w/underliner	65.00– 70.00
	#5	Same, amber	50.00– 60.00
Row 4:	#1	Pink	40.00– 45.00
	#2	Green w/liner	40.00– 50.00
	#3	Imperial, pink	45.00– 50.00
	#4	Imperial, pink w/floral cutting	40.00– 45.00
	#5	Same, green, plain	40.00– 45.00
Row 5:	#1	Paden City #198, 8 oz., amber	45.00– 55.00
	#2	Same, green	40.00– 45.00
	#3	Same, pink	40.00– 45.00
	#4	Paden City "Party Line," green	40.00– 45.00
	#5	Same, pink	40.00– 45.00
	#6	Paden City #198, 12 oz. green w/liner	50.00– 55.00

SYRUP PITCHERS (Continued)

Row 1:	#1	Crystal	20.00– 25.00
	#2	Green (possibly U.S. Glass)	40.00– 45.00
	#3	Standard Glass, pink	50.00– 55.00
	#4	Hocking, green swirl	40.00– 45.00
	#5, 6	Crystal, ea.	15.00– 20.00
Row 2:	#1	Amber/yellow combination w/glass lid	40.00– 45.00
	#2	Pink w/green knob, handle & pink underliner	55.00– 60.00
	#3	Duncan & Miller "Caribbean," blue	175.00–195.00
	#4	Same, crystal	60.00– 75.00
	#5	Cambridge, amber	40.00– 45.00
Row 3:	#1	Paden City, green floral cutting w/underliner	50.00– 55.00
	#2	Same, pink	55.00– 60.00
	#3	Same, pink w/painted flowers	40.00– 45.00
	#4	Cambridge, pink	50.00– 55.00
	#5	Paden City, forest green	30.00– 35.00
Row 4:	#1, 3	Cambridge etched design w/underliner, pink	65.00– 70.00
	#2	Same, green	65.00– 70.00
	#4	Same, amber	45.00– 50.00
	#5	Cambridge, etched "Cleo"	175.00–200.00
Row 5:	#1	Cambridge, "Tally Ho" amber	60.00– 65.00
	#2	Cambridge, pink	55.00– 60.00
	#3	Same, amber	40.00– 50.00
	#4	Cambridge, amber	45.00– 50.00
	#5	Crystal, with crystal top	20.00– 25.00
	#6	Fenton, black	100.00–125.00
Row 6:	#1	Heisey, "Moongleam" green	70.00– 75.00
	#2	Heisey, "Sahara" yellow	75.00– 85.00
	#3	Same, crystal	35.00– 40.00
	#4	Heisey, "Flamingo" pink	60.00– 70.00
	#5	Same, "Moongleam" green	55.00– 65.00
	#6	U.S. Glass miniature syrup, crystal	40.00– 45.00

WATER BOTTLES

There are many types of water containers shown throughout this book. People tend to think of plastic jugs as water containers today. Water bottles have gone the way of ice boxes which is where most of these were originally used.

The "RADIUM EMANATOR FILTER" bottle shown below is an interesting find. In its original McKee carton, there is an empty space where the radium filter was to have been placed. The set is made up of a 12" bottle (marked "Radium Emanator Filter Co., Inc., North Haledonn, N.J.) which turns up onto another 12½" bottle. The total filtering system stands 21" tall. The "Canary Yellow" color is called vaseline by collectors. This bottle set sells for $375.00–400.00.

Row 1:	#1	"Water Falls"	15.00– 18.00
	#2	"Water"	10.00– 12.00
	#3	"G.E." shows old refrigerator	15.00– 18.00
	#4	"Well," amber	75.00–100.00
	#5	"Ships"	15.00– 18.00
Row 2:	#1	Owen-Illinois "Juice" on one side & "Water" on other	8.00– 10.00
	#2	Forest green "Penguin"	15.00– 18.00
	#3	Lattice design w/lid	45.00– 50.00
	#4	Hocking "Royal Ruby"	175.00–200.00
	#5	"G.E." round	10.00– 12.00
Row 3:	#1	"Crisscross," crystal	20.00– 25.00
	#2	"The Well Informed Choose Ice Refrigeration"	8.00– 10.00
	#3	"Beveragette," Pat. 1919	15.00– 18.00
	#4	Cobalt blue, 64 oz., 10" tall	55.00– 60.00
	#5	Same, 32 oz.	55.00– 60.00

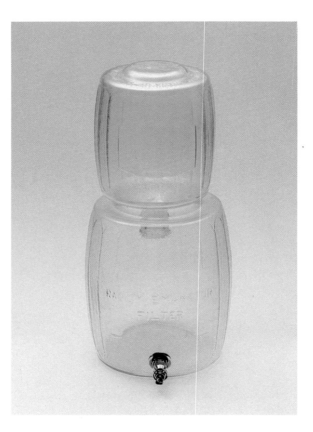

Part 3 – Patterns & Companies

"CRISSCROSS," Hazel Atlas Glass Company, 1936–1938

Collectors were first attracted to "Crisscross" because of the blue color. Now there are advocates for all colors including crystal. Crystal is often mixed with one of the other colors for a more varied appearance. Crystal prices have soared since the last book while the other colors have risen more slowly.

There are no new discoveries in this pattern, but the 5½" round bowl shown on page 207 is the piece presently eluding everyone. I have found a green lid, but no bottom.

Pink tumblers are elusive as are all colored sugars and creamers. No one has found a sugar and creamer in blue — yet. Nor have there been blue tumblers found to go with the pitchers. Those of you who collect other patterns of Depression era glass know how frustrating it is to collect a pattern that has a pitcher with no tumblers or vice versa.

Cobalt blue mixing bowls are just not being found! Many collectors are settling for bowls with use marks to have them at all. This has caused the prices for mint condition bowls to rise to the point that other collectors are settling for buying only the smaller mixing bowls and forgetting the two larger sizes.

One thing that confuses new collectors is the difference in the pound butter and the refrigerator dish that is like the butter. Look at the picture on page 207. The butter in Row 4 has a bottom that sticks out with tabs. The top of the refrigerator dish is flush with the edges of the bottom as seen in Row 3.

	Blue	Crystal	Green	Pink
Bottle, water, 32 oz.	—	20.00– 25.00	90.00–100.00	—
Bottle, water, 64 oz.	—	25.00– 30.00	100.00–125.00	—
Bowl, mixing set (5)	270.00–350.00	67.00– 90.00	135.00–160.00	130.00–160.00
Bowl, mixing, 6⅝"	30.00– 45.00	8.00– 12.00	18.00– 25.00	20.00– 25.00
Bowl, mixing, 7⅝"	40.00– 55.00	10.00– 15.00	20.00– 25.00	20.00– 25.00
Bowl, mixing, 8¾"	50.00– 65.00	12.00– 15.00	25.00– 30.00	25.00– 30.00
Bowl, mixing, 9⅝"	60.00– 75.00	15.00– 20.00	30.00– 35.00	30.00– 35.00
Bowl, mixing, 10⅝"	90.00–110.00	22.00– 28.00	40.00– 45.00	40.00– 45.00
Butter, ¼ lb.	95.00–115.00	18.00– 25.00	40.00– 55.00	35.00– 40.00
Butter, 1 lb.	95.00–115.00	20.00– 25.00	50.00– 55.00	50.00– 55.00
Creamer	—	15.00– 18.00	50.00– 55.00	50.00– 55.00
Food mixer (baby face)	—	35.00– 40.00	—	—
Pitcher, 54 oz.	700.00–800.00	110.00–125.00	—	—
Reamer, lemon	—	12.00– 18.00	25.00– 30.00	275.00–300.00
Reamer, orange	275.00–300.00	12.00– 18.00	25.00– 30.00	225.00–250.00
Refrigerator bowl, round 5½" w/cover	150.00–200.00	15.00– 25.00	135.00–150.00	140.00–150.00
Refrigerator bowl, w/cover				
4" x 4"	30.00– 40.00	8.00– 12.00	25.00– 30.00	25.00– 30.00
4" x 8"	80.00– 95.00	15.00– 20.00	40.00– 45.00	40.00– 45.00
8" x 8"	110.00–125.00	18.00– 25.00	50.00– 55.00	50.00– 55.00
Refrigerator dish (like butter),				
3½" x 5¾"	100.00–125.00	20.00– 25.00	60.00– 70.00	—
Sugar	—	15.00– 20.00	30.00– 35.00	30.00– 35.00
Sugar lid	—	25.00– 30.00	45.00– 50.00	40.00– 50.00
Tumbler, 9 oz.	—	30.00– 40.00	—	85.00–125.00

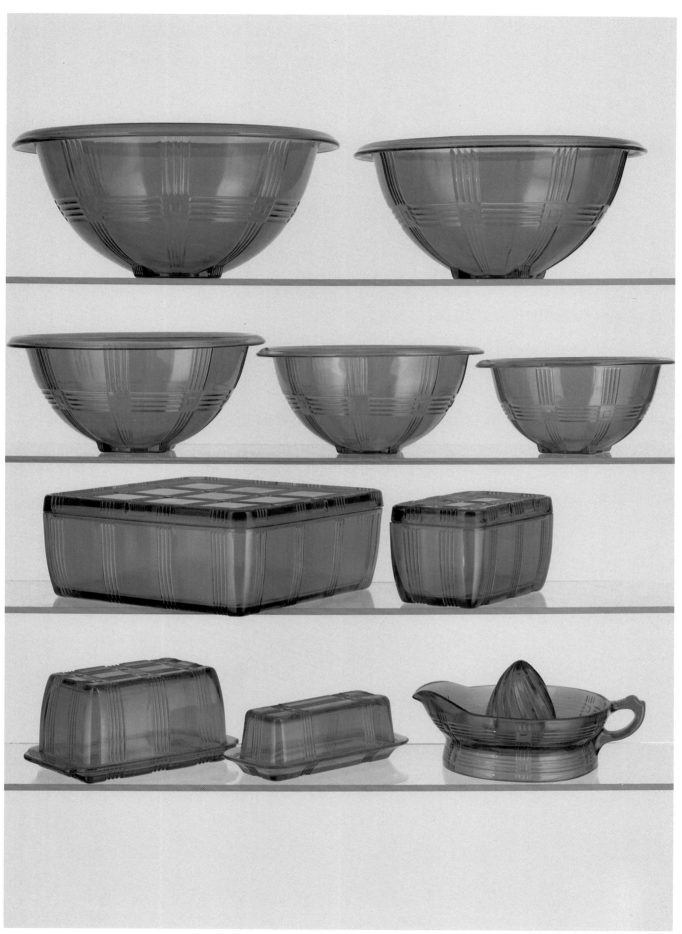

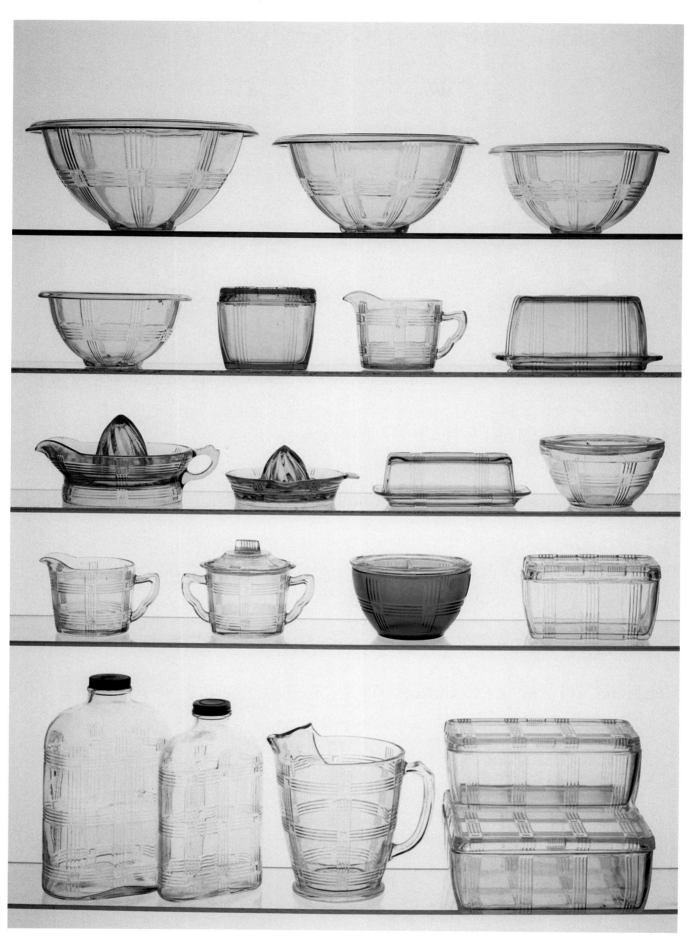

"DOTS," McKee Glass Company, 1930's – Early 1940's

McKee issued this as a "Deluxe" line of kitchenware and sold items to merchants from $4.00–12.00 per dozen. I have priced most items available although only a representative sampling can be seen on pages 209 and 211.

Page 209	Black/Green Dots on Custard	Blue/Red Dots on Custard	Dots on White
Bowl, 9", scalloped edge	30.00– 35.00	30.00– 35.00	22.00–25.00
Bowl, 9", w/spout	22.50– 25.00	25.00– 28.00	20.00–22.00
Bowl, drippings	30.00– 33.00	30.00– 35.00	20.00–22.50
Bowl, egg beater w/lip	20.00– 25.00	22.50– 25.00	15.00–17.50
Butter dish, 1 pound	100.00–125.00	100.00–125.00	45.00–50.00
Canister, 48 oz., screw lid	60.00– 65.00	65.00– 75.00	45.00–50.00
Canister, 28 oz., screw lid	45.00– 50.00	45.00– 50.00	35.00–40.00
Canister & lid, round, 48 oz.	22.50– 25.00	25.00– 28.00	20.00–22.00
Canister & lid, round, 40 oz.	20.00– 22.50	22.50– 25.00	18.00–20.00
Canister & lid, round, 24 oz.	18.00– 20.00	18.00– 20.00	12.00–15.00
Canister & lid, round, 10 oz.	15.00– 18.00	16.00– 18.00	12.00–15.00
Mixing bowl, 9"	16.00– 18.00	17.50– 20.00	12.50–15.00
Mixing bowl, 8"	15.00– 17.50	15.00– 17.50	12.00–15.00
Mixing bowl, 7"	12.00– 15.00	12.00– 15.00	10.00–12.00
Mixing bowl, 6"	10.00– 12.00	10.00– 12.50	8.00–10.00
Pitcher, 2 cup	35.00– 38.00	35.00– 38.00	25.00–28.00
Refrigerator dish, 4" x 5"	15.00– 18.00	15.00– 18.00	8.00–10.00
Refrigerator dish, 5" x 8"	20.00– 22.50	20.00– 25.00	15.00–18.00
Shaker, salt or pepper, ea.	15.00– 17.50	15.00– 17.50	12.00–15.00
Shaker, flour or sugar, ea.	22.50– 25.00	22.50– 25.00	18.00–20.00

"DOTS," Hazel Atlas & Hocking Glass Companies '30's – '50's

Dot designed kitchenware was made by several companies. The later made Fire-King "Dots" can be found in red, gold and black. These Dot designs are becoming very popular patterns with collectors, although red "Dots" seems the more coveted color. It's been dubbed "Measles" by collectors!

Page 210

Row 1: #1 Hazel Atlas bowl, 9", red — 18.00–20.00
#2 Same, 8" — 15.00–18.00
#3 Hazel Atlas pitcher, 2 cup — 35.00–38.00
#4 Pitcher, ribbed 2 cup — 25.00–30.00
Row 2: #1 Hazel Atlas bowl, 8", yellow — 15.00–18.00
#2 Same, 6" — 10.00–12.00
Same, 7" (not shown) — 12.00–15.00
#3 Red, 5" — 8.00–10.00
#4 Hocking grease jar — 18.00–25.00

Row 3: #1 Hocking red bowl, 9$\frac{1}{2}$" — 12.00–15.00
Same, 8$\frac{1}{2}$" (not shown) — 10.00–12.00
#2 Same, 7$\frac{1}{2}$" — 8.00–10.00
#3 Same, 6$\frac{1}{2}$" — 5.00– 6.00
Row 4: #1 Hocking "Apple," 9$\frac{1}{2}$" — 12.00–15.00
Same, 8$\frac{1}{2}$" (not shown) — 10.00–12.00
Same, 7$\frac{1}{2}$" (not shown) — 8.00–10.00

FIRE-KING Anchor Hocking Glass Company, Late 40'S – 60's

An assortment of Dots is shown here along with Anchor Hocking's popular "Tulips" design. Grease jars and the designed "Tulips" shaker tops (without rust and damage) are becoming scarce.

Page 211

Row 1: #1 McKee refrigerator dish, 4" x 5" 18.00–25.00
#2 McKee 24 oz. round canister w/lid — 20.00–25.00
#3 Anchor Hocking 7$\frac{1}{2}$" gold "Dots" bowl — 12.00–15.00
Row 2: #1 Red "Dots" 8" bowl — 15.00–18.00
#2 Yellow "Dots" 6" bowl — 10.00–12.00
#3 Brown "Dots" 5" bowl — 8.00–10.00
Row 3: #1 "Banded Dots" 8$\frac{1}{2}$" blue bowl 12.00–15.00
#2 Same, 7" yellow bowl — 10.00–12.00

Row 3: (Continued)
#3 Pyrex "Art Deco" casserole 75.00–100.00
Row 4: #1 "Tulips" bowl, 9$\frac{1}{2}$" — 12.00– 15.00
#2 Same, 8$\frac{1}{2}$" — 10.00– 12.00
#3 Same, 7$\frac{1}{2}$" — 8.00– 10.00
Row 5: #1 Same, 6$\frac{1}{2}$" — 6.00– 8.00
#2 Same, grease jar — 20.00– 22.00
#3 Same, shaker — 7.50– 10.00
#4 Batter bowl, "Fruits" (peaches, grapes and pears) — 20.00– 25.00

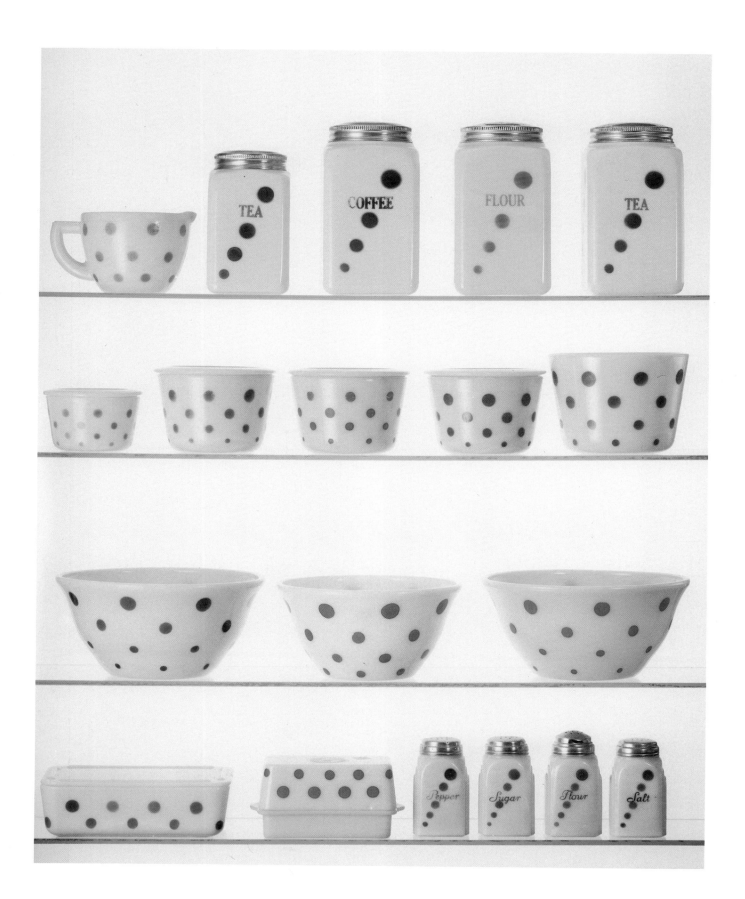

FIRE-KING

Page 213

Row 1: #1 Pink Floral, casserole, 1 qt. 10.00–12.00
  #2 Same, 4" refrigerator dish 3.00– 4.00
  #3 Same, 8" bowl 10.00–12.00
  #4 Same, 5 oz. low custard 2.50– 3.00
  #5 Fruit, 5 oz. low custard 2.50– 3.00
  #6 Fruit, 8 oz. mug 6.00– 8.00
Row 2: #1 "Splash Proof," "Turquoise Blue,"
   9½" mixing bowl, 4 qt. 15.00–18.00
   Same, 8½", 3 qt. (not shown) 12.00–15.00
  #2 Same, 7½", 2 qt. 10.00–12.00
  #3 Same, 6½", 1 qt., 10.00–12.00
  #4 7½" gold "Dots" bowl 8.00–10.00
Row 3: #1 "Swedish Modern," "Turquoise Blue,"
   11" mixing bowl, 3 qt. 18.00–20.00

Row 3: (Continued)
  #2 Same, 9½", 2 qt. 15.00–17.50
  #3 Same, 8", 1 qt. 12.50–15.00
  #4 Same, 6½", 1 pt. 10.00–12.00
Row 4: #1 "Ivory," 9" cake pan 12.00–14.00
  #2 Same, 9⅛" deep loaf pan 10.00–12.00
  #3 Same, 10½" baking pan 12.00–15.00
Row 5: #1 Silver decorated casserole,
   signed "Georges Briard" 20.00–25.00
  #2 Pedestal Ivory cake plate 6.00– 8.00
  #3 Forest Green batter bowl 12.50–15.00
  #4 Forest Green, 6½", 1 qt. bowl 8.00–12.00

Page 214

Row 1: #1 "Modern Tulip" 3 qt.
   mixing bowl 10.00–12.00
  #2 Same, 4 qt. 12.00–15.00
  #3 Same, 2 qt. 8.00–10.00
  #4 Same, 1 qt. 6.00– 8.00
Row 2: #1,3 "Modern Tulip" salt and
   pepper pr. 15.00–18.00
  #2,5 "Modern Tulip" or Apples
   and Cherries grease jar 20.00–25.00
  #4 "Kitchen Aids" 2 qt. mixing bowl 8.00–10.00
Row 3: #1 Fleur-de-lis Leaf, bowl, 7" 6.00– 7.00
  #2 Same, 6" 5.00– 6.00

Row 3: (Continued)
  #3 Same, 5" 4.00– 5.00
  #4,5 Grecian scene tumbler
   (showing front and back), ea. 6.00– 7.50
  #6 Same, ice bowl 10.00–12.00
Row 4: #1 Souvenir mug, Patton Museum,
   Ft. Knox, Ky. 6.00– 8.00
  #2-5 Water Lily sherbet, ea. 2.00– 3.00
  #6 Esso "Tony the Tiger" mug 6.00– 8.00
Row 5: #1 Basket weave 4" bowl 1.50– 2.00
  #2 Chicken and Fruit, 1 qt. casserole 5.00– 8.00
  #3 Same, 2 qt. 7.00– 10.00

FIRE-KING, Sapphire Blue

Page 215

Baker, 1 pt., round or square	8.00– 10.00
Baker, 1 qt.	12.00– 15.00
Baker, 1½ qt.	10.00– 12.00
Baker, 2 qt.	12.00– 15.00
Bowl, 5⅜", cereal or deep dish pie plate	12.00– 15.00
Bowl, 4⅜", individual pie plate	12.00– 15.00
Bowl, 16 oz. measuring, 2 spout	22.00– 25.00
Cake pan (deep), 8¾"	20.00– 22.00
Casserole, 1 pt., knob handle cover	12.00– 15.00
Same, 1 qt.	12.00– 15.00
Same, 1½ qt.	12.00– 15.00
Same, 2 qt.	18.00– 20.00
Casserole, individual, 10 oz.	10.00– 12.00
Casserole, 1 qt., pie plate cover	15.00– 18.00
Same, 1½ qt.	15.00– 18.00
Same, 2 qt.	18.00– 20.00
Coffee mug, 7 oz., 2 styles	22.00– 25.00
Cup, 8 oz., dry measure, no spout	200.00–250.00
Cup, 8 oz. measuring, 1 spout	18.00– 20.00
Cup, 8 oz measuring, 3 spout	20.00–22.00
Custard cup, 5 oz.	2.00– 3.00
Custard cup, 6 oz., 2 styles	2.50– 3.50
Loaf pan, 9⅛" deep	20.00–22.00
Nurser, 4 oz.	15.00–18.00
Nurser, 8 oz.	25.00–30.00
Pie plate, 8⅜"	8.00–10.00
Pie plate, 9"	9.00–10.00
Pie plate, 9⅝"	10.00–12.00
Pie plate, 10⅜", w/juice saver rim	80.00–90.00
Percolator top, 2⅛"	3.50– 5.00
Refrigerator jar & cover, 4½" x 5"	15.00–18.00
Same, 5⅛" x 9⅛"	25.00–30.00
Roaster, 8¾"	40.00–45.00
Roaster, 10⅜"	60.00–65.00
Table server, tab handles (hot plate)	18.00–20.00
Utility bowl, 6⅞"	12.00–15.00
Utility bowl, 8⅜"	15.00–18.00
Utility bowl, 10⅛"	18.00–20.00
Utility pan, 8⅛" x 12½"	20.00–22.00

MIXING BOWLS

	PACKING
G4100/1 —4 Pce. Mixing Bowl Set	6 sets — 41 lbs.
(Each Set in Gift Carton)	
G4100/54—4 Pce. Mixing Bowl Set	2 doz. —140 lbs.
(Bulk Packed in 6 Cartons)	sets
G4100/66—4 Pce. Mixing Bowl Set	8 sets — 48 lbs.
(Each Set Nested & Packed in an Individual Cell)	

The Sets listed above consist of one each of the G4156, G4157, G4158 and G4159 Bowls.

OPEN STOCK

G4156—6" Mixing Bowl	2 doz. —	18 lbs.
G4157—7" Mixing Bowl	2 doz. —	26 lbs.
G4158—8" Mixing Bowl	1 doz. —	20 lbs.
G4159—9" Mixing Bowl	1 doz. —	28 lbs.

	PACKING
G300/129—3 Pce. Mixing Bowl Set	2 doz. — 68 lbs.
(Bulk Packed in 3 Cartons)	sets

COMPOSITION: One each 4 7/8", 6" and 7 1/4" Bowls

OPEN STOCK

G355—4 7/8" Mixing Bowl	2 doz. —	13 lbs.
G356—6" Mixing Bowl	2 doz. —	21 lbs.
G357—7 1/4" Mixing Bowl	2 doz. —	34 lbs.

"MODERN TULIP" DECORATION

RANGE SET

W300/244—4 Pce. Range Set
Each Set in Gift Carton, 8 Sets to Shipping Carton — 19 lbs.
COMPOSITION: One Salt Shaker—White Top
One Pepper Shaker—White Top
One Range Jar & Cover

The above Range Set and matching Mixing Bowl Sets in "Modern Tulip" decoration, are not available in Open Stock.

W300/242—3 Pce. Mixing Bowl Set
Each Set Nested & Packed in an Individual Cell,
8 Sets to Shipping Carton — 44 lbs.
COMPOSITION: One 1 Qt. Mixing Bowl
One 2 Qt. Mixing Bowl
One 3 Qt. Mixing Bowl

W300/243—4 Pce. Mixing Bowl Set
Each Set in Gift Carton, 4 Sets to Shipping Carton — 37 lbs.
COMPOSITION: One 1 Qt. Mixing Bowl
One 2 Qt. Mixing Bowl
One 3 Qt. Mixing Bowl
One 4 Qt. Mixing Bowl

HEAT-PROOF

MIXING BOWLS

		PACKING	
W4100/5	—4 Pce. Mixing Bowl Set	6 sets	— 41 lbs.
	(Each Set in Gift Carton)		
W4100/55	—4 Pce. Mixing Bowl Set	2 doz.	—150 lbs.
	(Bulk Packed in 6 Cartons)	sets	
W4100/67	—4 Pce. Mixing Bowl Set	8 sets	— 48 lbs.
	(Each Set Nested & Packed in an Individual Cell)		

The Sets listed above consist of one each of the
W4156, W4157, W4158 and W4159 Bowls

OPEN STOCK

W4156—6"	Mixing Bowl	2 doz.	— 19 lbs.
W4157—7"	Mixing Bowl	2 doz.	— 29 lbs.
W4158—8"	Mixing Bowl	1 doz.	— 22 lbs.
W4159—9"	Mixing Bowl	1 doz.	— 29 lbs.

		PACKING	
W300/130—3 Pce. Mixing Bowl Set		2 doz.	— 66 lbs.
	(Bulk Packed in 3 Cartons)	sets	

COMPOSITION: One each 4⅞", 6" and 7¼" Bowls

OPEN STOCK

W355—4⅞"	Mixing Bowl	2 doz.	— 13 lbs.
W356—6"	Mixing Bowl	2 doz.	— 20 lbs.
W357—7¼"	Mixing Bowl	2 doz.	— 33 lbs.
W358—8⅜"	Mixing Bowl (Not Illustrated)	1 doz.	— 27 lbs.

"KITCHEN AIDS" DECORATION

RANGE SET

W300/239—4 Pce. Range Set
    Each Set in Gift Carton, 8 Sets to Shipping Carton — 19 lbs.
COMPOSITION: One Salt Shaker—White Top
                One Pepper Shaker—White Top
                One Range Jar & Cover

The above Range Set and matching Mixing Bowl
Sets in "Kitchen Aids" decoration, are not
available in Open Stock.

W300/237—3 Pce. Mixing Bowl Set
    Each Set Nested & Packed in an Individual Cell,
    8 Sets to Shipping Carton — 44 lbs.
COMPOSITION: One 1 Qt. Mixing Bowl
                One 2 Qt. Mixing Bowl
                One 3 Qt. Mixing Bowl

W300/238—4 Pce. Mixing Bowl Set
    Each Set in Gift Carton, 4 Sets to Shipping Carton — 37 lbs.
COMPOSITION: One 1 Qt. Mixing Bowl
                One 2 Qt. Mixing Bowl
                One 3 Qt. Mixing Bowl
                One 4 Qt. Mixing Bowl

HEAT-PROOF

FRY GLASSWARE, H.C. Fry Glass Company, 1920's–1930's

The opalescent white color most people are familiar with was called "Pearl" by the factory. Decorated pieces are more desirable than the regular issues. All colors are rarer than the "Pearl" with both blue shades ("Azure" {light} and "Royal" {cobalt}) the most in demand. Fry glass without an opalescent effect is called "lime glass." According to avid Fry collectors, ovenware condition is not as important as obtaining an important addition to a collection.

All dates or numbers listed are marked on the piece.

Page 219

Row 1: #1 Reamer, fluted, jello mold, "Canary" 275.00– 300.00
#2 Meat loaf w/lid, rectangular, 9" 55.00– 65.00
#3 Reamer, straight side 300.00– 325.00
Row 2: #1 Grill plate, 8½", "Rose" 25.00– 30.00
#2 Same, "Azure" blue 30.00– 40.00
#3 Measure cup, 3 spout, "Pearl" 65.00– 75.00
#4 Bean pot w/lid, 1 pt. 65.00– 75.00
Row 3: #1 Grill plate, 10½", "Rose" 40.00– 45.00
#2 Measure cup, 1 spout 60.00– 70.00
#3 Grill plate, 10½", "Pearl" w/blue trim 50.00– 65.00
Row 4: #1 Same, w/orange enamel trim 50.00– 65.00
#2 Reamer, straight side, "Azure" blue 1,500.00–1,750.00

Row 4: (Continued)
#3 Same as #1, "Royal" blue 50.00– 65.00
Row 5: #1 Meat platter, 13", green, "Not Heat Resisting Glass" 80.00– 85.00
#2 Percolator top w/blue finial 30.00– 35.00
#3 Snack plate, 6" x 9", w/cup "Royal" blue 60.00– 70.00
Row 6: #1 Same as Row 5 #1, 17" 100.00–110.00
#2 Percolator top w/green finial 25.00– 30.00
#3 Casserole, oval, 7", w/green trim 85.00– 95.00

Page 220

Row 1: #1 Domed roaster (1946-14) 14" x 10" x 7½" 175.00–195.00
#2 Same as #1 but in metal holder. Paper label reads: "This is a 'ROYALLOY' Steel Frame. Dry thoroughly after using and it will serve you well and long." 175.00–200.00

Row 2: **Sunnybrook Cookie Jar** (Introduced at $0.57; original price $0.75)
#1 "Royal" blue 250.00–275.00
#2 Green 175.00–225.00
#3 "Rose" 175.00–200.00
#4 Black 250.00–275.00

Page 221

Row 1: #1 Bean pot w/lid, 1 qt. in holder 95.00–110.00
#2 Cream soup, 5¼", ftd. 50.00– 55.00
#3 Casserole w/lid, 8" round, in holder 30.00– 35.00
Row 2: #1 Casserole, oval, 10" w/green finial 95.00–110.00
#2 Sundae glass "MACO-MFG-CO, VAPOR-RITE, MAY-WOOD-ILL 50.00– 55.00
#3 Oval platter, 9" x 13" 35.00– 40.00
Row 3: #1 Casserole, 6" round 25.00– 30.00
#2 Baker, 6" round 22.00– 25.00
#3 Cocotte, 5" (for indiv. meat, chicken, oyster pies) 15.00– 20.00
#4 Same, 4" 15.00– 20.00
#5 Custard cup, 4½ oz. 8.00– 10.00
Row 4: #1 Snack plate, 6" x 9" w/cup 30.00– 35.00
#2 Mushroom baker/round shirred egg, 6" 100.00–125.00

Row 4: (Continued)
#3 Baker, oval, 6" 25.00– 30.00
#4 Apple baker or custard, 4¾" 25.00– 30.00
Row 5: #1 Butter pat (?) "Fry's Heat Resisting Glass" 50.00– 75.00
#2 Ramekin, 3" 8.00– 10.00
#3, 4 & 7 Custard cup, 4 or 6 oz. (1927 or 1936) 8.00– 10.00
#5, 6 Custard cup, 6 oz., engraved (1927 or 1936) 10.00– 12.00
Row 6: #1 Casserole, 7" round, engraved w/blue finial 110.00–125.00
#2, 3 Ramekin "Pearl" or "Lime glass," ea. 8.00– 10.00
#4 Oval server, 8 sided, engraved, 6½" x 9"/holder 60.00– 65.00

FRY GLASSWARE, H.C. Fry Glass Company 1920's–1930's (Continued)

The antique business is a conduit to meeting many interesting collectors from all over the country. At the Heisey Convention in 1988, I met a couple of avid Fry collectors on preview night. I would like to thank Hank and Carla Bowman for the use of their Fry glassware for this section as well as for providing valuable information for use in the book. Hopefully, I will be able to go back to California for photographs for the next book.

Most people in all collecting fields are more than willing to share glass and information. That is one of the more rewarding aspects of writing. I hope you gain knowledge to help your collecting from the long hours spent compiling this.

Row 5 consists of a child's set that was sold for $2.50 in 1922. It was called "Little Mother's Kidibake Set" and now sells for $300.00.

Page 223

Row 1:	#1	Casserole w/lid, 7" square, in holder	55.00–65.00
	#2	Baker, pudding, 2$\frac{1}{8}$" x 6$\frac{3}{8}$"	25.00–30.00
	#3	Casserole w/lid, 8" oval, engraved in holder	40.00–45.00
Row 2:	#1	Brown betty, 9"	50.00–55.00
	#2	Casserole w/lid, 7" round, engraved side & lid	50.00–55.00
		Trivet, 8" under casserole	17.50–20.00
	#3	Shirred egg, 7$\frac{1}{2}$", round	20.00–25.00
Row 3:	#1	Vegetable dish, 2 part, 9$\frac{3}{4}$"	30.00–35.00
	#2	Fish platter, 11", engraved	45.00–55.00
	#3	Pie plate, 9$\frac{1}{2}$", engraved, in holder	30.00–35.00
Row 4:	#1	Cake, 9" round	25.00–30.00
	#2	Cup and saucer, No. 1969	40.00–45.00
	#3	Pie plate, 10" in metal holder	20.00–25.00
Row 5:	#1	Pie plate, 5"	60.00–65.00
	#2	Casserole w/lid, 4$\frac{1}{2}$" round	85.00–95.00
	#3,4	Ramekin, 2$\frac{1}{2}$", ea	30.00–40.00
	#5	Bread baker, 5"	70.00–75.00
Row 6:	#1	Fish platter, 17", engraved	50.00–60.00
	#2	Casserole w/lid, 7" round, embossed w/grapes	55.00–65.00

"JENNYWARE," Jeannette Glass Company, 1936-1938

"Jennyware" is popular with collectors due, in part, to the many different items that can be acquired. A major problem in collecting "Jennyware" is the variations of color occurring in ultra-marine. The greenish shade of "Jennyware" has few collectors. Dealers usually avoid buying that shade for resale.

That decanter in the top row was made by Imperial and is not a part of the "Jennyware" set. Many collectors buy it as a "go-with" item. It sells for $40.00-50.00.

Page 225, 226

	Crystal	Pink	Ultramarine
Bowl, mixing set (3)	50.00– 60.00	120.00–130.00	120.00–130.00
Bowl, 10½"	20.00– 25.00	50.00– 55.00	45.00– 55.00
Bowl, 8¼"	15.00– 20.00	40.00– 45.00	40.00– 45.00
Bowl, 6"	10.00– 15.00	25.00– 30.00	25.00– 30.00
Butter dish, deep bottom	110.00–125.00	150.00–175.00	150.00–175.00
Butter dish, flat bottom	——	——	200.00–250.00
Coaster	——	6.00– 8.00	6.00– 8.00
Measuring cup set (4)	1,50.00–170.00	195.00–215.00	195.00–215.00
1 cup	40.00– 45.00	55.00– 60.00	55.00– 60.00
½ cup	40.00– 45.00	50.00– 55.00	50.00– 55.00
⅓ cup	35.00– 40.00	50.00– 55.00	50.00– 55.00
¼ cup	35.00– 40.00	40.00– 45.00	40.00– 45.00
Pitcher, 36 oz.	85.00– 95.00	110.00–125.00	110.00–125.00
Reamer	85.00–100.00	110.00–125.00	110.00–125.00
Refrigerator dish, 70 oz., round	25.00– 30.00	55.00– 65.00	55.00– 65.00
Refrigerator dish, 32 oz., round	20.00– 25.00	45.00– 50.00	45.00– 50.00
Refrigerator dish, 16 oz., round	15.00– 20.00	40.00– 45.00	40.00– 45.00
Refrigerator dish, 4½" x 4½"	12.00– 15.00	22.00– 25.00	22.00– 25.00
Refrigerator dish, 4½" x 9"	18.00– 20.00	30.00– 32.50	30.00– 32.50
Shaker, footed, ea.	12.00– 15.00	20.00– 25.00	22.00– 25.00
Shaker, flat, ea.	20.00– 25.00	30.00– 35.00	——
Tumbler, 8 oz.	22.00– 25.00	35.00– 40.00	40.00– 45.00

Pyrex, Corning Glass Works

Delphite blue Corning glassware is beginning to attract more American collectors. Canadian collectors have been aware of it for years.

Page 227

Row 1:	#1	Blue 12" Pyrex, square based bowl		20.00– 25.00
	#2	Blue 10" pie plate		18.00– 20.00
	#3	Blue divided relish		20.00– 22.50
Row 2:	#1	Crystal Pyrex measure cup		12.50– 15.00
	#2	Pyrex "Clambroth" white oval casserole		100.00–125.00
	#3	Pyrex red refrigerator dish		100.00–125.00
Row 3:	#1	Mixing bowl , 8½"		12.00– 14.00
	#2	Mixing bowl , 7½"		10.00– 12.00
	#3	Mixing bowl , 6½"		8.00– 9.00
Row 4:	#1	Pyrex 9 piece "Economy Set" #179 consisting of 8 oz. measuring cup, 9½" pie plate, six 4 oz. custards & handy cup rack		30.00– 35.00
	#2	Pyrex 8 piece "Matched Set" #145 consisting of six 5 oz. custard cups, one 1½ qt. casserole w/pie plate cover in box		25.00– 30.00
Row 5:	#1, 2	Boxes for sets pictured, ea.		4.00– 5.00

"SHIPS," McKee Glass Company, 1930's

Collectors still prefer white lids for their canisters; but if you use these, the clear tops are more convenient for viewing the contents of the dish! Black or red "Ships" are priced similarly. There seems to be more red available than black. All those different "Drippings" containers make you think that there were many grease jar set promotions "back then."

Page 229

Bowl, drippings, 8 oz.	35.00–40.00	Mixing bowl, 9"	18.00–20.00
Bowl, drippings, 16 oz.	35.00–40.00	Mixing bowl, 8"	15.00–18.00
Bowl, drippings, rectangular (4" x 5")	35.00–40.00	Mixing bowl, 7"	12.00–15.00
Bowl, egg beater w/spout, 4½"	40.00–45.00	Mixing bowl, 6"	10.00–12.00
Bowl, beater w/spout, 6½"	30.00–35.00	Pitcher, 2 cup	30.00–35.00
Butter dish	30.00–35.00	Refrigerator dish, 4" x 5"	18.00–20.00
Canister & lid, round, 48 oz., 5"h	35.00–40.00	Refrigerator dish, 5" x 8"	20.00–22.00
Canister & lid, round, 46 oz., 4½"h	35.00–40.00	Shaker, salt or pepper, ea.	10.00–15.00
Canister & lid, round, 24 oz., 3½"h	22.00–25.00	Shaker, flour or sugar, ea.	18.00–20.00
Canister & lid, round, 10 oz., 2½"h	20.00–22.00	Tumbler (or Egg Cup)	20.00–22.00
Mixing bowl set (4)	55.00–65.00		

"SHIPS" and "DUTCH"

These categories are more related than you think. They share the same cabinets at home. Cathy collects both of these, and they are fun to find. You never know what unusual piece will surface. Cathy enjoys them, so I look for them in my travels, hoping not to find a big grouping miles from the car.

Page 230

Row 1: #1 Jadite, 9¾" bowl, w/windmills — 45.00–50.00
  #2, 3 Hocking canister w/Dutch decal, ea. — 15.00–20.00
  #4 Hocking provision jar w/Dutch decal — 12.50–15.00
Row 2: #1 Windmill "Drippings" (turned wrong) — 30.00–35.00
  #2 Dutch boy shaker — 10.00–12.50
  #3 Dutch boy and girl shakers w/holder — 15.00–18.00
  #4 "Churn lady" pr. shakers — 15.00–18.00

Row 2: (Continued)
  #5-7 Tipp City Dutch shakers, ea. — 6.00– 7.00
Row 3: #1 Black "Ships" beater bowl, 6½" — 30.00–35.00
  #2 Same, 10 oz. canister — 18.00–20.00
  #3 Same, 24 oz. — 20.00–22.50
  #4 Same, 46 oz. — 25.00–27.50
Row 4: #1 Same, refrigerator dish, 5" x 8" — 22.50–25.00
  #2 Same, 4" x 5" — 17.50–20.00
  #3 Same, 6" mixing bowl — 10.00–12.00

"DUTCH," "DUTCH," and more "DUTCH"

Page 231

Rows 1 & 2: **Hazel Atlas "Skating Dutch"**
  #1 One piece stack set — 20.00–22.50
  #2 Three piece stack set — 35.00–38.00
  #3 Mixing bowl, 9" — 12.50–15.00
  #4 Same, 8" — 10.00–12.00
Row 2: #1 Same, 7" — 7.50–10.00
  #2 Same, 6" — 8.00–10.00
  #3 Same, 5" — 6.00– 8.00
  #4 Cereal bowl, 5" — 6.00– 8.00
  #5 Salt and pepper pr. — 16.00–18.00

Row 3: #1 Dutch/tulips/windmills, 9" mixing bowl — 12.50–15.00
  #2 Same, 8" — 10.00–12.00
  #3 Same, 7" — 7.50–10.00
  #4 Same, 6" — 8.00–10.00
Row 4: #1 Same, 5" — 6.00– 8.00
  #2 Fired-on Dutch set w/holder, 3" — 25.00–30.00
  #3 Same set, 4" — 35.00–40.00

LATE ARRIVALS and REPRODUCTIONS

Due to the time lapse between the fourth and fifth editions of this book, several miscellaneous photos were taken at different times. I concluded it was better to have the pieces shown in some form than not at all.

Page 232 50th Anniversary Plate 10.00–12.00

Page 233

Row 1:
#1 Hocking pretzel mug, crystal w/colored stripes 10.00–15.00
#2 Glasbake light yellow measure cup 25.00–30.00
#3 "Midget" washer 12.50–15.00
#4 Red curtain tie back 12.50–15.00
#5 Federal amber butter tub 25.00–30.00

Row 2:
#1 Crystal etched oil and vinegar 22.50–25.00
#2 Blue tie back 12.50–15.00
#3 Percolator part 10.00–12.50
#4 Forest Green cruet 35.00–40.00
#5 Sugar dispenser 12.50– 15.00

Row 3:
#1 Duncan "Festive" gravy boat and ladle 50.00– 55.00
#2 Cake plate and cover 50.00– 55.00
#3 McKee turquoise 6" bowl 35.00– 40.00
#4 Syrup 18.00– 20.00

Row 4:
#1 McKee Chalaine blue 7¼", sq. 110.00–125.00
#2 Same 6¼", sq. 90.00–100.00
#3 Straw holder, zippered design 75.00–100.00
#4 Amethyst straw holder 100.00–125.00
#5 Cocktail shaker, cut leaf band 12.50– 15.00

Page 234

Row 1:
#1 Glass iron 500.00–600.00
#2 Cambridge cobalt blue salad set 250.00–300.00

Row 2:
#1, 3 Shakers, patriotic "God Bless America"; "It's Great to be an American" 15.00– 17.50
#2 Butter dish, Lincoln picture 35.00– 40.00

REPRODUCTIONS – BARNES REAMERS

This picture shows the colors of Barnes (made for Edna Barnes of Uniontown, Ohio) reamers issued as of December 1988. THESE ARE LIMITED EDITION REAMERS. They are collectible in their own right. Some colors are sold out and are selling above the issue price. Three additional colors have been made since 1989. They are pink carnival, milk blue, and opal blue.

Page 235

Rows 1-3: See pages 146 – 147 for original colors. Both the top (inside cone) and the bottom (on the base) are marked with a **B** in a circle. A few of the cobalt blue are marked with an N and not a B, so be aware of that. These will be listed in order they were made. (Some are satinized or frosted).

#1 Cobalt — Row 1, #1
#2 Rubina — Row 2, #3
#3 Vaseline & frosted — Row 1, #2, 3
#4 Black — Row 3, #1
#5 Apple green & frosted — Row 2, #1, 2
#6 Cranberry Ice & frosted — Row 1, #4, 5
#7 Gold & frosted — Row 2, #4, 5
#8 Blue Bell & frosted — Row 3, #2, 3
#9 White Milk & painted blue & painted pink flowers also — Row 3, #4, 5
#10 Aqua & frosted (not shown)
#11 Red (not shown)

Rows 4-8: Show Barnes reamers which are called 5" and 2½", but really measure 4¾" and 2¼". There is a **B** in a circle on the tab handle of both sizes. Some of these have also been frosted.

Row 1: Heatherbloom, Custard, Green Carnival, Forest Green
Row 2: Cobalt, Sapphire, Harvest Swirl
Row 3: Cranberry Ice, Gold, Pink Rosemarie
Row 4: Red Glow, Depression Green, Chocolate
Not shown: Milk Blue

REPRODUCTIONS and NEWLY MADE ITEMS

When I wrote the third edition of *Kitchen Glassware,* there were only a few Kitchenware items to report as reproductions. With the demise of Westmoreland Glass Company and the sale of their glass moulds, a whole new world of reproductions appeared. I will approach each item shown on page 237 separately. These are all new! If you wish to purchase any of these, you need to realize that the price for newly made items is determined by seller demand and what the buyer is willing to pay. There is little structured market price especially on the "foreign" made "rip-offs."

Do not be surprised at any color appearing in these items whether it is pictured or not! Know your dealer if you do not know the merchandise! Subscribe to a national trade paper to keep abreast of the latest happenings. (See page 240.)

Row 1: #1-3 – Westmoreland w/oranges and lemons being made by Summit Art Glass in colors of black, "Moonlight" blue, cobalt blue, and "vaseline." Original moulds are being used and only pink, green, and crystal were made originally.

Row 1: #4, 5 – Hazel Atlas 2 cup reamer being made in Far East (likely Taiwan) in green, cobalt blue and pink. THIS IS A MAJOR PROBLEM! Even reamer collectors are having difficulty with this one. The green is easily seen by the horrible color; the pink and blue are fairly true to the originals. They are good copies! The repros all have an oily slick feel and are slightly heavier than the older ones. The repros are wavy and lettering on the sides is slightly different. However, it is impossible to tell you a sure way to tell the old from the new in words so you can feel safe in buying these. I can only emphasize to know who you are dealing with and if the price seems reasonable on an expensive piece, then there might be a good reason. **BUYER BEWARE!**

Row 2: #1-4 – Easley pat. July 10 1888, Sept 10, 1888. Never made in color originally. Original crystal sells $12.00–15.00.

Row 2: #5 – Hazel Atlas cobalt blue three spout, one cup measuring cup made in Taiwan. Spouts are not smoothly made, but it is a good copy.

Row 2: #6 – Hazel Atlas "Kellogg's" embossed cup was made in green and pink in Taiwan. Major difference is on the number 4 in 4 oz. measurement on side. In old, line forming 4 crosses in **middle** of 4 while on new, the perpendicular line crosses ¾ of the way down the 4 in the 4 oz.

Row 3: #1-5 – Gillispie cup w/reamer top made by Summit Art Glass. Cup was never made in color and originally had a measure top instead of reamer top. (See page 117.)

Row 3: #6, 7 – Dry measure w/reamer top made by Summit Art Glass but heretofore, unknown.

Row 4: #1, 2 – Hazel Atlas shakers (salt and pepper) made in Taiwan. Never made in cobalt blue originally. Pink quality varies greatly as do designs. Stippling effect behind embossed salt or pepper is very pronounced on new. New tops are punched in circular pattern.

Row 4: #3 – Fostoria "Colony-like" two spout reamer made originally in white and crystal.

Row 4: #4-7 – Duboe Pat. July 24, 1917, made by Summit and copied without markings in Taiwan. Never made in color originally and sells $40.00–50.00 in crystal.

Row 5: #1-4 – Made by Summit Art Glass from Westmoreland mould. Original colors are shown on page 165 in Rows 3-5. All additional colors are NEW!

Row 6: #1, 3 – Same as dry measures in Row 3: #6, 7 but spout pulled to make measure cup.

Row 6: #2 – Possible Westmoreland cup, footed and spouted and made by Summit in black.

Row 6: #4 – Same as Row 2 without reamer top.

Row 6: #5, 6 – Cobalt blue and black made for Barnes by Imperial in 1981. (Marked IG 81)

LATE ARRIVALS

At the end of our six day photography session last October, we had the following pieces left that didn't make it into other photographs, so here they are! In Row 3 #2 is a pink item that in the past has been sold as a napkin holder. It is part of a Cambridge desk set!

Page 238
Below: Paramount napkin holder from side and front angles. 400.00–450.00

Page 239
Row 1:	#1	Pryex, 9" bowl	8.00–10.00
	#2	Same, 7" bowl	5.00–6.00
	#3	"Handi-Serv Decanter, copyright 1951 General Foods Corp."	5.00–6.00
	#4	Paden City yellow iced tea	10.00–12.50
Row 2:	#1	Pyrex, $3^1/2$" x $4^3/4$" refrigerator bowl	5.00–6.00
	#2	Pyrex, 6" bowl	4.00–5.00
	#3	Percolator top, cobalt blue	18.00–20.00
	#4	Pyrex, 8" bowl	7.00–8.00
	#5	Westmoreland, reamer, 2 part, ice blue	155.00–175.00
Row 3:	#1	Butter dish, quarter pound, pink	40.00–50.00
	#2	Glasbake meat platter	10.00–12.00
	#3	"Napkin holder" (piece from Cambridge desk set)	25.00–30.00
	#4	Hazel Atlas pink pint canning jar	20.00–25.00
Row 4:	#1	Fork, blue handle (Goes with spoon on page 177)	27.50–30.00
	#2,3	Amber salad set w/crystal handles	30.00–35.00
	#4	Imperial amber spoon	27.50–32.50
	#5	Fry 13" meat platter, pink, "Not Heat Resisting"	70.00—80.00
	#6	U.S. Glass cake stand or bowl cover	12.50–15.00

A publication I recommend:

DEPRESSION GLASS DAZE

P.O. Box 576F, Otisville, MI 48463

A monthly newspaper devoted to the collecting of colored glass (depression glass & china) – features ads, articles, prices, news pertaining to this hobby. (12 issues)

Name _____

Address _____

City _____ State ____ Zip _____

New   1 Yr. $21.00   Free Sample Copy
           2 Yrs. $40.00   Canada $22.00

Books By Gene Florence

Collector's Encyclopedia of Akro Agate Glassware $14.95

Collector's Encyclopedia of Depression Glass $19.95

Collectible Glassware from the 40's 50's 60's $19.95

Pocket Guide to Depression Glass $9.95

Collector's Encyclopedia of Occupied Japan I $14.95

Collector's Encyclopedia of Occupied Japan II $14.95

Collector's Encyclopedia of Occupied Japan III $14.95

Collector's Encyclopedia of Occupied Japan IV $14.95

Collector's Encyclopedia of Occupied Japan V $14.95

Elegant Glassware of the Depression Era $19.95

Very Rare Glassware of the Depression Years Third Series....................$24.95

Very Rare Glassware of the Depression Years Fourth Series.................$24.95

Very Rare Glassware of the Depression Years Fifth Series.....................$24.95

Stemware Identification..$24.95

Add $2.00 postage for the first book,
30¢ for each additional book.

Copies of these books may be ordered from:

Gene Florence

Web Page: http://members.aol.com/GFlore829/GeneFlorence

or

Collector Books
P.O. Box 3009
Paducah, KY 42002-3009